YIDDISHLAND

GÉRARD SILVAIN   HENRI MINCZELES

YIDDISHLAND

GINGKO PRESS

First published in the United States of America in 1999
by Gingko Press, Inc.
5768 Paradise Drive, Suite J
Corte Madera, CA 94925
tel: 415-924 9615
fax: 415-924 9608
email: gingko@linex.com

ISBN: 1-58423-018-5

English edition edited by Donna Wiemann
Thanks to Bill Dworkin

Copyright 1999 Editions Hazan, Paris
Translated from the French by David Wharry
Printed in Spain

Design: Atalante, Paris
Production: Maya Masson
assisted by Claire Nau
Editor: Juliette Hazan
Corrector: Bernard Wooding
Color separation: Prodima, Bilbao
Printing: I.G. Castuera, Pampelune

CONTENTS

A JOURNEY INTO THE HEART OF YIDDISHLAND

Goodnight vast world
Giant world, stinking world
[...]
And even though all has been devastated
I am searching for the dust in your dust
Desolated Jewish life
Jacob Glatstein

"There is a land which figures on no map of the world, a strange, unknown land 7
of almost unreal immensity, whose ever-changing frontiers traverse continents and
oceans. It is the land of Yiddish. How many claim this language as their own, from
New York to Moscow, from Buenos Aires to Warsaw, from Jerusalem to Paris, from
Melbourne to Johannesburg? Millions."

The words of Haim Sloves, a committed writer and playwright in Yiddish. Thanks to the countless postcards that Gérard Silvain has collected, it is this geographical and cultural world we are going to visit, without passport or visa, without fear of being turned away, simply by turning back the clock with an ardent desire to rediscover a Jewish civilization which for centuries has forged an entire people and given it its specificity and originality.

The question is whether Yiddishland is a mythic country or not. It has no capital, no government, no ministers, offices, administration or bureaucracy. It is a cultural concept emanating from Yiddish, a Jewish language spoken by around eleven million people on the eve of the Second World War. Yiddishland was, quite simply, the land where Yiddish was spoken. Around the Yiddish language, there was Yiddishkeit, a pluralist cultural amalgam. Yiddishland was more than a country, it was an unknown continent.

The key words are Yiddish, Yiddishland, Yiddishkeit, and also Yiddishophone, Yiddish speaker and Yiddishist (the Yiddish militant and standard-bearer).

YIDDISHLAND, OR THE YIDDISH HOMELAND

With the ukase of December 31st, 1791, Catherine the Great created a zone of residence—some spoke of a zone of containment—for the Jews. The territory, with an area of around one million square kilometers, was in the west of Russia, stretching from the Baltic Sea to the Black Sea. The Jews called it "the Pale" and they remained under house arrest there for more than a hundred and forty-five years. The zone was not abolished until after the revolution of February 1917.

Yiddishland represented 12% of the total population of the sixteen provinces or governments over which it spread, to which one must add the ten governments of Poland after the Congress of Vienna in 1815. Within the Pale's enforced boundaries, a Yiddish-speaking environment developed throughout the 19th century, despite the precarious living conditions (the city of Kiev, in the middle of the residential zone, was forbidden to Jews). However, for about fifteen years during the liberal reign of Alexander II, Yiddishland was allowed to develop and many Jews obtained access to universities and Russian schools. From 1859 onward, the most wealthy merchants were able to establish themselves in Moscow and St. Petersburg.

In 1791, the residential zone had a population of one and a half million. Around seven million Jews, more than 95% of them Yiddish speakers, lived there just before the Russian Revolution.

In the last century and up until the 1940s, Yiddishland, both a mythical and real land and cradle of Yiddish in the Old World, was situated in eastern Europe. Poland was considered the crucible, the hub of a Yiddish world which stretched from the west of the ex-Soviet Union, from the Ukraine and Belorussia through Romania, Bessarabia and eastern Hungary to the Baltic states. Its principal centers were Warsaw, Lodz, Lvov, Kraków, Vilnius, Minsk, Odessa, Kishinev, Iasi, and the countless towns with a majority Jewish population, known in Yiddish as *shtetlach*. Other centers grew up around the "periphery": between 1880 and 1930, millions of Jews, fleeing the pogroms, insecurity and poverty, left for central and western Europe and the United States, Latin America, South Africa and Australia. Yiddish-speaking communities developed in Vienna, Berlin, London, Antwerp, Brussels, Paris, Johannesburg, Buenos Aires and Melbourne. The greatest number crossed the Atlantic to the United States. At the turn of the century, New York was the largest Yiddish center in the world. The Yiddish language became the substitute for the lost homeland. It became a country which transcended frontiers and geography. It was the intellectual luggage Jews took with them all over the world.

Ideological excesses and the tragedies of war produced unexpected tribulations. Jewish communities grew up in Birobidzan, the Soviet state created from scratch in the Far East by Stalinists turned into "Zionists without Zion," and, during the Second World War, in Shanghai, Kobe, Kharbine, Samarkand and Tashkent, where war caused the Jews to flee to save their lives.

To describe Yiddishland, one must talk about Yiddish, the language of the Jews of these regions. In *Berechit*, Roland Doukkan wrote: "Yiddish! Do you realize, here is a people, therefore a language, which people want to disappear, just like that. Disappeared: streets, whole quarters, villages, the names over the doors of the little shops, ways of eating, laughing and praying! The holocaust is all this as well, not just millions of dead. It is this will to make everything disappear, puff! in one fell swoop, to decree that suddenly all has ended, that there will be nothing left except a few names on a monument here and there, in Jerusalem or elsewhere! Later, one day, a descendant may translate a text or a poem, but the language itself, the tongue used to buy bread, to say hello how are you, that language will remain buried in books which only old people still open from time to time. Nearly all the newspapers have gone up in smoke, and so Yiddish has become like Sanskrit and Maya or the language of the Pharaohs. It took thousands of years to kill off those languages, whereas Yiddish..."

Yiddishland had its good periods. In the 18th century, in greater Poland under the administration of the Council of Four Lands (*Vaad arba aratsot*), Jewish communities enjoyed genuine cultural, institutional and religious autonomy. Between the two World Wars, the Polish Jews, classified as a national ethnic minority under the Treaty of Versailles, benefited from this specific status despite vicissitudes and state anti-Semitism.

But other periods were infinitely more unstable. Despite flourishing temporarily in the Soviet Union after the 1917 revolution, Yiddish, like so many other minority tongues, was smothered by Stalin. This culminated in the five-year paroxysm of the Shoah, the great catastrophe, the summit of horror and abomination during which six million men, women and children, most of them Yiddish speakers, were exterminated. Yiddish was assassinated. It is now a buried, hardly accessible language. The number of Yiddish speakers today is estimated at barely one million. Enclaves remain where the *mame loshn* is still spoken and taught: the Yiddish-speaking communities of Paris and New York, Oxford University, the ultra-religious communities in Borough Park in Brooklyn, the Mea Shearim in Jerusalem. It is still spoken by the Litvaks of Tel Aviv and Johannesburg, by the retired couples of Florida and the scattered survivors of the Shoah wherever they are, most of whom are now more than sixty years old, and of course by a few fanatic lovers of the language and Yiddish culture.

Jewish society was above all a collective community which, to quote Rachel Ertel, "had at stake the elaboration of a specific existence." She adds: "This is why all these aspirations, including the most universal ones, from the Haskala (The Enlightenment) to the various Zionist movements and Socialism and Communism, are part of a historical continuity. History is perhaps the only real Jewish territory. It is in history that culture, whose roots have been driven down into the depths and density of time, has met with political expediency."

For several centuries, Yiddish, a profane language, was used to explain and comment on the holy writings, the Bible and the Talmud, written in Hebrew or Aramaic. Men of letters and learned people understood Hebrew, the language of study and communication of Jews dispersed all over the world. At the same time, because they were an ethnic minority, the Jews spoke to various degrees and more or less frequently and fluently the language of the host country. Bilingual or trilingual Jews were not rare. In intellectual circles in Lithuania, Warsaw or Odessa, families conversed in Yiddish, Hebrew, Russian, Polish and German at will. In Kovno, in Emmanuel Levinas's family, everyone spoke Hebrew, Russian and German.

In the 19th century, as a result of the Enlightenment, there was a renaissance of Hebrew, which in turn had become a profane language. In Kovno, Vilnius and Odessa, a neo-Hebraic literature was founded whose principal exponents were Abraham Mapou, Isaac Baer Levinsohn, Judah Leib Gordon and Peretz Smolenskin. Some writers, including Mendele Mokher Sefarim and

Sholem Aleichem, began writing in Hebrew, their mother tongue, then switched to Yiddish, both out of personal conviction and a desire to reach a wider readership.

For a thousand years, Yiddish was the principal language of the Ashkenazi Jewish communities established in Germany and France post Charlemagne and which spread east during the following centuries, introducing a Germanic language into the Slavic world. It is the only Jewish language apart from Hebrew to have taken root despite—some say thanks to—its dispersion. Judeo-German, derived from several Germanic dialects in the Middle Ages and written in Hebrew script, became the everyday language of the Jews and, after undergoing several mutations, became known as Yiddish—from *taytsh* (German) and *yiddish* (Jewish). Having borrowed words from other languages, particularly from Slavic and Judeo-Roman tongues, and having incorporated international terms, modern Yiddish contains a majority of terms of German origin, 5 to 10% Slavic and 15 to 20% Hebrew. Language of fusion (*Shmeltzshprakh*) par excellence, it has constantly "Yiddishized" foreign words and terms.

In Yiddishland, the Yiddish language was the principal vehicle of Jewish identity, and of both religious tradition and secular modernity, together with their cultural and political ramifications. Max Weinreich, director of the Yiddish Scientific Institute (YIVO) in Vilnius, pointed out that even though Yiddishland was a territory without borders, army or flag, Yiddish had its metaphysical army and fleet. According to him, the army was its readers and the navy its journalists, that is to say the *Oylem* (the people, the multitude). In Hebrew this word is *Olam*, which also means eternity.

Yiddishland was made of people: rabbis, intellectuals and public figures respected in the community for their erudition, but also the multitude, the humble, the small and the simple. Jewish intellectuals belonged to what was known in western Europe as the intelligentsia—the term intellectual was coined in the West during the Dreyfus Affair. The *intelligenti* were, above all, reformers. On a political level, during the last third of the 19th century, they were violently opposed to racial, religious and nationalist oppression, as were the young Jews who struggled against Tsarist autocracy. Some of them became revolutionaries, others—like Ahad Ha'am (Hebrew: "One of the People"), the founder of spiritual Zionism—joined the ranks of the Zionists or, like Eliezer Ben Yehuda, created the modern Hebrew state or became leaders of Poale Zion (Workers of Zion) like Ber Borokhov. Some discarded the cosmopolitanism of the period and became Yiddishist Jews: the language, it was hoped, would ensure the future for the Jewish people. Chaim Zhitlowski is an exemplary representative of this tendency. A leader like Charles Rappoport, who espoused all the ideologies of the Left, he claimed to speak ten languages fluently, all with a Yiddish accent. One must not forget Ludwik Zamenhof, who in 1887 "forged" Esperanto, an international language designed to supplant national tongues. All these men and women struggled with the complexity of a world in mutation.

There were many such leaders, but it was the "pocheter yidn," the ordinary, uncomplicated Jews, who formed the immense majority. They were known as the "popular masses," a term which has disappeared from our vocabulary because it is too ideological. Today, we have a tendency to employ socio-professional denominations. Often, in popular imagery, and above all in the eyes of non-Jews, to be Jewish meant one was a peddler or a usurer. In reality, Jews exercised many manual crafts: tanning, shoe-mending, water carrying, knitting, watchmaking, ironwork, etc. At the beginning of the century, the French hatter's guild was largely made up of immigrant Jews, one of whom, Alexandre Lozovsky, became a well-known union leader and an apparatchik of the Third International. It was also said that in western Europe at the end of the last century there were so many Jewish tailors they could have dressed half the inhabitants of the Russian empire.

There were also the workers and porters with callused hands—often called the *shtarke* (well-built)—who waited to be hired for odd jobs, or the *balgole* (carters and coach drivers) who, rain or shine, transported people from one *shtetl* to another. Along the roads were Jewish taverns which fed Jews and *goyim* (gentiles) alike. Jewish farmers, more numerous than is thought, in Lithuania and Crimea particularly, formed small isolated collectives of *yeshuvniks*. They were located near *shtetls* of some importance and respected the religion of their non-Jewish neighbors. The Yiddish writer Zalmen Schneour immortalized a colorful character, Noah Pandre, whose panache deliberately broke the typical stereotype of the Jew as a coward. One recalls similar characters in the books of Sholem Asch, in which, for example, the butchers and the *shokhtim* (ritual cattle slaughterers) of Kolo Street stood up against the pogromists.

The *shtetl*, abundantly described by Yiddish writers, was a majority Jewish village or small town of between a thousand and twenty thousand inhabitants. The *shtetl* conjures up a warm, nostalgic image steeped in folklore. There were countless *shtetlekh* in Poland, Russia, Lithuania and Romania. However, despite the bucolic descriptions, the folksy images and a nostalgia for a lost world forever frozen in memory, the reality was very different. The *shtetl* was racked by poverty and misery, without hope or future. It was frozen in secular traditions which little by little woke up to the echoes coming from the outside, evolving world and which eventually destabilized it. The heart of *shtetl* society was the home (*Yiddish Heim*), around which there was the synagogue (*bet ha-midrash*) and the community with its cultural and social activities and its commercial lung, the market square. This micro-society was more or less identical from one *shtetl* to another.

Industrialization, the emergence of an upper middle class and the birth of a class of workers and craftsmen entirely transformed the sociological and economic structure of the *shtetlekh*. Their future became doubtful and their population dwindled. Many young people went to the large towns or abroad, attracted by better living conditions. According to Rachel Ertel, the *shtetl* was a meeting place of tradition and modernity and beneath "the semblance of torpor, it was like a pressure cooker." Although it had its own guilds (*khevrot*), its own mutual aid brotherhoods and study societies, it was never completely self-sufficient. Noises from the outside world resonated in each village and accentuated its politicization.

THE SOUND AND THE FURY OF THE TOWNS

The people of the *shtetlach* discovered the towns, a world of movement and mutation. They left the dirt tracks and found themselves in streets, in a landscape of factories, sweatshops and workshops, in a grim new reality of work, cramped lodgings, misery and promiscuity. The Jewish quarters were either confined to the town centers or pushed out to the edges. The town of Lodz, 150 kilometers south of Warsaw, mushroomed in the middle of a textile region. It was known as the Polish or Jewish Manchester. The Jewish population of Lodz grew from eleven in 1793 to two hundred and twenty thousand in 1939, a third of the town's majority German and Polish population.

In the second half of the 19th century, Lodz grew from twenty-five thousand to three hundred thousand inhabitants. Workshops became huge factories such as Poznanski, where 6,300 people worked. In *The Brothers Ashkenazi*, Israel Joshua Singer, the elder brother of Isaac Bashevis Singer, winner of the Nobel Prize for literature in 1978, described the grim existence of the Jewish proletariat. They worked inhumanly long hours for a pittance in a world of soot and smoke, families of ten children or more living cramped together in large grey buildings on the outskirts of Balut. In 1914, more than twenty-seven thousand Jewish workers were employed in the textile industry. In the inner and outer suburbs, in Zdunska Wola or Pabianice, people worked at home, owning one or more looms and working around a hundred hours a week.

Lodz was a large urban center. Outside its residential quarters stood a drab dormitory town whose squares, courtyards, workshops, shops, esplanades, and grid of avenues nevertheless had a certain charm. When you meet people who were born in Lodz, they talk about it passionately. They spent their adolescence, their youth there.

In Lodz, Jewish social, cultural and political life was extraordinarily rich. There was a dense fabric of charitable, educational, sports, artistic and literary institutions. Remember that the first barricades under the Russian empire were erected there in June 1905. Poles and Jews fought side by side. Remember also the Lithuanian rabbi Elia Hayim Meisel, the famous leader of the Jews of Lodz during the 1910s. Let us also not forget that in 1944 the poet Itzhak Katzenelson wrote the moving *Song of the Assassinated Jewish People* there. And remember also that Haim Rumkowski, the much written about megalomaniac, remained *Judenältester* (head of his ghetto) until it disappeared.

Warsaw, on the Vistula River, has been capital of Poland since it replaced Kraków in the 16th century. Renamed Warschau under the German occupation, Varche has for five hundred years been a home for Jews and they have contributed greatly to the city's commercial and political development.

From the first Jewish inhabitants right up until the partition of Poland, the Jewish community of Warsaw underwent periods of exclusion, discrimination and expulsion. In 1792, at the time when the Jewish Legion was formed under the leadership of Berek Yoselwicz, the Jewish population was 6,750, 10% of the total population.

Warsaw, a bastion of Polish nationalism, was in turn hostile and welcoming, but this did not prevent the Jewish community from growing considerably. In contrast to Vilnius, which was an important religious center, Jewish Warsaw opened up more quickly to outside influences. Just before the Second World War, Warsaw's 370,000 Jewish inhabitants could be proud of a rich heritage of writers, thinkers, philosophers, academics and journalists, a school system, a vigorous press and highly structured political parties, all of which were powerful forces behind the Yiddish language.

Certain strata of the bourgeoisie and the liberal professions, more integrated into Polish culture, lived in quarters all over the capital, but the majority of the Jewish population lived in the central Nalewski quarter, in streets with melodic names like Grzybowska, Mila, Nowolipie, Dzika and Ciepla. In each building, with its rectangular courtyard, its shops with Yiddish signs, lived hundreds of families, every one of them Jewish except the concierge's.

In 1941, the Jewish population of Warsaw, which had already been persecuted on several occasions, was around a half a million men, women and children, of which eighty-three thousand died of starvation, cold and epidemics, in particular typhoid. At the height of the occupation, in the face of overwhelming adversity, the Jews succeeded in maintaining a vibrant cultural life. Each new day was a day of terror but also of hope. The revolt of the ghetto in April 1943 took the Nazis and the free world by surprise. The people of the ghetto had given meaning to their death. They died "for their liberty and for ours."

***

In the northern border region, Vilna (Russian), Wilno (Polish), Vilnius (Lithuanian) and *Vilné, Yerushalaym de Lita* (Yiddish) was called the Jerusalem of Lithuania by Napoleon. In 1940, eighty thousand of its two hundred thousand inhabitants were Jewish and the town enjoyed enormous prestige. In the Zydowska quarter, in the heart of the city, stood the Shulhoyf, with its accompanying social and cultural facilities.

Jews had settled in the town since the 14th century, encouraged by the Lithuanian grand dukes because of their professional and commercial qualifications. Despite many vicissitudes, they contributed to the town's renown. Thanks to rapid industrialization in the second half of the 19th century, Vilnius, at the heart of this hinterland, established itself as a crossroads between western and eastern Europe.

It was in Vilnius, or *Heimshtot* (our town), or *Ir Vaem be Israel* (the metropolis of Israel), that Elia Zalman, the *gaon* of Vilnius, the *mitnagged* (the opposer), pronounced his *kherem* (excommunication) of the Hasidim, rejecting their mysticism and reaffirming the importance of the rigorous study of the scriptures. Count Valentine Potocki, a Polish nobleman and convert to Judaism who refused to renounce his new faith, was burnt at the stake there. Vilnius was the birthplace of the Bund (General Union of Jewish Workers) and of the Zionist workers' movement. It was the seat of YIVO and had a well-known art school where Soutine and several painters of the Jewish school of Paris studied. Vilnius was immortalized by three poets, the Pole Czeslaw Milosz, the Lithuanian Tomas Venclova and the Yiddishist Avrom Sutzkever. Tzemakh Shabad was a legendary doctor of the poor there. It was the home of Zalmen Reizen, one-man band, linguist, journalist, and theorist of Folkism (Jewish autonomism). Dr Yakub Wigodzki was uncontested president of the Kehilla. Vilnius was the heart of Yiddishland, perhaps even its spiritual capital, and claimed also to be the center of Litvakland, a local minority of the Ashkenazi Jews and a cultural concept which, to a greater or lesser extent, included Litvak rationalism and the pureness of the language.

Vilnius was the Jerusalem of ghettos, whose inhabitants, under terrible conditions, managed to develop their own cultural specificity, while the town's other citizens knew full well that they would inevitably be taken to Pouar, only a few kilometers away, where over seventy thousand of them were murdered.

Odessa, on the shores of the Black Sea and the commercial, agricultural and industrial lung of the Ukraine, attracted the Jews quite late. It was not until the end of the 18th century that the first Jews arrived, coming mostly from the country, in particular from Bessarabia. Less than a hundred in 1795, a hundred years later they numbered seventy-five thousand and, on the eve of the Second World War, one hundred and ninety thousand, 30% of the total population. Jewish craftsmen, shopkeepers, wholesalers, industrialists, bankers, professional people, manual and office workers and the Jewish proletariat cramped in the inner suburbs all played a vital role in the town's growth. It was a first-rate intellectual center and the home of writers in Yiddish (Mendele Mokher Sefarim), Hebrew (Nachman Bialik) and Russian (Isaac Babel). It was also a political center. Jewish socialists distinguished themselves during the 1905 and 1917 revolutions. There were prominent Odessa Zionists, including Leon Pinsker in the 1880s, Ahad Ha'am, Ber Borokhov, Menakhem Ussishkin, Vladimir Jabotinsky and the historian and autonomist Simon Dubnov.

Odessa, with its docks, prostitution and organized crime, was a city of variety and paradox: the Menshevik Julius Martov's grandfather, the *maskil* (adept of the Haskala) Rabbi Alexander Tzederbaum, founded the Jewish newspaper *Hamelitz* and two other Yiddish publications, *Kol Mevasser* and *Yiddishes Folksblat*; the manifesto of protest by the Russian intellectuals against the pogrom of Kishinev in 1903 was headed by Tolstoy as well as by Jews; Anna Lifchitz, at the height of the revolution, violently criticized the Tsar; and there was the lovable knave and gang leader, Benia Krik. It was a proud, generous, warm town whose Mediterranean climate contrasted with the rigorous winters of continental Russia. Odessa harbor was the theater of the mutiny of the *Potemkin* and the location for Eisenstein's movie. The murderous Nazi regime and its Romanian accomplices wiped out a rich and tumultuous past, today hidden beneath a grey veil of monotony. 17

***

Moving north, we reach Minsk where, from the end of the 14th century, coming from the east, the first Jewish families arrived in the rapidly expanding town. Five centuries later, Minsk had forty-seven thousand Jewish inhabitants, 52% of the total population.

Its increasing industrial role in the textile industry (flax and wool) and in engineering (tractors and machine tools) made it a merchant city of repute, at the crossroads between East and West. At the beginning of the 20th century, the Jewish community had a large number of religious institutions and, in the 1920s, secular schools. Minsk socialist groups vied with neighboring Vilnius for the lead in revolutionary activity. In the 1880s and 1890s, Minsk was the seat of the Lovers of Zion and Poale Zion (Workers of Zion), who preached rigorous ideological pureness and accepted only the option of a return to Palestine, refusing all others, particularly Uganda.

Minsk was also an important center of Yiddishism after the revolution, under the rule of the Jewish version of communism, Yevsektsyia. At the beginning of the 1930s, however, it went into decline, the prelude to a nightmare which saw the closure of the Jewish Scientific Institute, whose linguistic section was the pride of its researchers. The year 1948 saw the beginning of a cultural genocide, with the murder of the actor Solomon Mikhoels, followed, on August 12th, 1952, by the assassination of the Yiddish-speaking intelligentsia in Moscow.

During the invasion of Russia by Germany in 1941, one hundred and fifty thousand Jews, some of whom had fled from Poland and Lithuania, were rounded up in Minsk. For two years, their life was an unending hell. Mass executions by the Einsatzkommando, the mobile death squads of the SS, and the Wehrmacht and their local auxiliaries accounted for the deaths of more than one hundred thousand Jews. However, active resistance by partisans in the ghetto and the surrounding forests, under the command of Hersz Smolar, in liaison with the clandestine movement in Belorussia, struck serious blows against the Nazis.

There was also Kraków, Lublin, Lvov, Czernowicz and many other towns. Today, despite the will to survive, to re-establish a cultural life and to preserve what in Yiddish is called *hemshekh* (continuity), there are only three thousand Jews in Lodz, five thousand in Warsaw, four thousand in Vilnius, twenty thousand in Odessa and fifteen thousand in Minsk. These survivors are the guardians of a civilization brutally razed to the ground.

In order to describe this martyrdom, resuscitate these obliterated communities, and remember those who disappeared, several hundred commemorative books (*Yizker Bikher*) have been published. They are monuments to the past, the paper tombstones of buried towns, and represent the duty of those who survived to never forget.

THE GOD OF ISRAEL

In the *Dictionnaire encyclopédique du judaïsme,* Sylvie-Anne Goldberg wrote: "What is Judaism? History, a religion, an identity, a label, a memory, a people, a law, a book?" It is all of these.

If Yiddishland embodied the Jews' oneness with a land, a territory, Yiddishkeit expressed their attachment to the rules of life laid down by religion. To immerse oneself in Yiddishkeit was to absorb all its commandments, the *mitzvot,* which fundamentally differentiated a Jew from a non-Jew. Until the First World War, Yiddishkeit meant to live as a Jew among Jews.

For centuries, to be a Jew meant first and foremost to subscribe to the law of Moses, to the Torah, and to observe the 613 commandments (*mitzvot*), codified by the *Shulhan 'arukh* (Prepared Table) of Yozef Caro. From birth to death, from the *heder* (school for small children) to the grave, a Jew's entire existence was regulated right down to the smallest detail.

Eight days after birth, the male child underwent his first initiation right, the *bris* (circumcision), by which he entered the Alliance and thereby became a Jew. From the earliest age, the young child was prepared for study. All day, from Sunday morning until midday on Friday, the Jewish child, in the *heder* (class), under the strict and sometimes brutal direction of a *melamed* (teacher), learnt the rudiments of tradition and recited the ritual prayers. Little by little, he mastered *ivrit* (Hebrew). When he had reached the upper *heder* and had been questioned by a *lamdn* (scholar), if he proved himself to be an *ilui* (genius) or a *talmid khokhem* (a brilliant pupil), he was sent to the *yeshiva* (Talmudic academy) where he could become either a man of letters—someone who, even when he married and became the father of many children, would still go on studying all his life—or, if he wanted, he could become a rabbi, i.e. a master and a teacher.

Aged thirteen, the Jewish child crossed the threshold of official maturity. With the celebration of the Bar Mitzvah he could become part of a *minyan* (an assembly of ten men for prayer). Then came marriage (*khasene*), symbol of joy and accomplishment, the achievement of fullness, the celebration that was expected to ensure the continuity of the Jewish people. True, marriages were often arranged in advance by *shadkhan* (marriage brokers), who were frequently depicted in Yiddish literature. The dowry was fixed, the *yikhes* (the family lineage) was consulted, meetings were arranged and, if required, a marriage contract (*ketuba*) was drawn up. At which point the *badkhen* (jester) appeared, followed by the *klezmorim* (the Jewish orchestra), composed of itinerant musicians who went from *shtetl* to *shtetl* celebrating the marriages of the *khosn* and the *kale* (bride and bridegroom) and chanting Mazel Tov to all the *mishpokhe* (family). The powerful and melodious voice of the *hazzan* (cantor) resounded in the bedecked synagogue. And then life carried on. Children were born and people died and were obligatorily buried in the Jewish plot of the cemetery.

For a long time, Jews lived in a cocoon from which they derived force and fervor. Every day, they said the morning prayer, the afternoon prayer and

Maariv, or evening prayer. This ritual symbolized the Jew's love of God. Its accoutrements were the *tsitsit,* or fringes of the *tallit* (prayer shawl), the *tefillin,* or small square boxes (phylacteries) with sheaths containing parchments with passages from the Torah—one of the little leather sheaths is fixed to the forehead, the other on the left arm—and finally the *mezuza,* another parchment scroll in a sheath, fixed to the right of the front door of the house. Meals, with their blessings and ritual graces, were strictly kosher (prepared according to nutritional laws whereby one does not mix meat and milk). The Jewish housewife played a vital role. Guardian of the family's Judaic identity and good housekeeper (*balboste*), she oversaw the children's education and even earned money for the household if her husband was too occupied with his studies. Jewish life was controlled by the Jewish calendar, which consisted of twelve or thirteen lunar months, alternately twenty-nine and thirty days long. Shabbat was the high point of the week. Elected by God, the Jew was lord of his own home, an uncontested patriarch who breathed Judaism among his own.

20   Whether historical or religious, Jewish celebrations were manifestations of each Jew's devotion to God. In the autumn, the year began with Rosh Hashana, the New Year and the anniversary of the Creation of the World, followed ten days later by Yom Kippur, day of fasting, atonement, forgiveness, prayer and penitence. After the gravity of the "Redoubtable" or "Terrible Days" came the joy of Sukkot (Feast of Tabernacles), followed by Simhat Torah (Rejoicing of the Torah), a wild saraband which the young and the not-so-young danced with fervor in the decorated *shul* (synagogue).

In December came Hanukka (the inauguration of the Temple), the fight for identity but also a party for children, who received presents of sweets and small change. *Latkes* (fried grated potatoes) were eaten. At Purim, everyone dressed up in fancy dress and took part in the *Purim-spil* (Purim games) in which Aman is defeated. On this occasion, "Aman's ears" (*Homenstashn*) were eaten.

Then came Pesah (Passover). Every Jewish home was spring-cleaned from top to bottom to banish any impurities (*hametz*), the bed linen was changed and the walls repainted. It was the festival of spring, the Yom Tov (day of celebration) par excellence. United around the head of the family, during the *seder* everyone ate *matzot* (unleaven bread) and read and commented on the Haggada (story) in which, according to the ritual, it is recalled that the Jews, then slaves in Egypt, were "the following year free men in the land of Israel."

Seven weeks after Pesah came Shavuot (Pentecost), close to the summer solstice and the harvest festival, and then finally, in July/August, Tisha be-Av, day of the destruction of the Second Temple in the year 70 AD and the most painful day of the Jewish calendar.

The Jewish religion was not simply strict observance of ritual but a whole code of behavior, a lifestyle, and those who strayed from it had to face the most punishing ordeals. In the 18th century, the religion underwent modifications. Hasidism, a pietistic doctrine which originated in Galicia and was propagated by Israel Ba'al Shem Tov, the Master of the Good Name, spread across the whole of eastern Europe. It became a popular movement and its ascension was irresistible. The simplicity and spirituality of this new mysticism produced a genuine revolution in people's hearts. Through its joyous fervor, prayer became a real remedy to the hardness of the times. But the new creed came up against the rationalist rigor of the *mitnagdim* (those in opposition), led by the charismatic *gaon* (spiritual leader) of Vilnius, Elia Zalman, who stressed the importance of Talmudic teaching and rabbinic study. With the following generations, things returned progressively to normal again, both camps peacefully refusing to give ground. In Germany at the beginning of the last century, under the influence of the Jewish Enlightenment (Haskala), Judaism became "confessionalized" and, under the guidance of Moses Mendelsohn, embraced more liberal tendencies.

Little by little, he forsook Yiddish for German and, seeking symbiosis with German culture, according to Heinrich Heine, bought his "entry ticket to European society." Such was not the case in eastern Europe, which managed to preserve its Jewish identity while opening itself up to modern ideas.

And so there was cohabitation between a religious orthodoxy—of which Agudat Israel was the dominant example before becoming its political arm—and Hasidism and more liberal religious movements. It was in this context that the first signs of a renaissance of the Jewish nation appeared and materialized into "nationalist" movements believing in Jewish autonomy within the Diaspora, and nationalist movements which favored a Jewish state whose languages were Yiddish and modern Hebrew.

THE IRRUPTION OF POLITICS

At the beginning of the 20th century and above all between the wars, Yiddishland gradually became secularized. *Weltlekhkeit* is not just the Jewish word for secularism. It also means universality, adapting the language to contemporary knowledge by the incorporation of new political and social terms. With industrialization, ancient structures dominated by the Kehillot, which provided the cohesion of the Jewish community in each town, broke up. The *kahal* (council) with its executive, its *bet din* (court of justice) and its religious, social aid, charity, public works, education and economy departments, had to withstand the wind of modernism that was sweeping the continent. The German Haskala and the ideals of the French Revolution—liberty, equality, fraternity—had finally penetrated the Yiddish world.

Under the combined influence of Russian populism and German Marxism, many young Jews were won over to socialism, especially as they had to struggle against both economic oppression and state anti-Semitism. The fight against economic oppression included the revolt against inhuman working hours (ten to twelve hours a day) and derisory pay. The fight against anti-Semitism meant forcefully protesting against the massacres and killings organized by the government. The Jews were designated as scapegoats for the population's discontent. The wave of pogroms in central Russia in 1881 caused an unprecedented exodus to America. But at the same time, in radical circles it was decided to oppose the Black Hundreds with military force. The beginning of the century saw the emergence of the Boevie Otriady, heroic gangs who had become specialists in urban guerrilla warfare and who inspired the Hagana before the creation of a Jewish state in 1948. For the first time in eighteen centuries, Zionist and socialist self-defense groups gave as good as they got.

As a result of a refusal to accept the passivity of a large proportion of the population, and in order to protest against economic exploitation, mutual aid funds (embryonic unions) and Jewish Social Democrat groups were formed in the 1890s. They formed federations and in 1897 created the first Jewish socialist party in Vilnius, the Union of Jewish Socialist Workers of Poland, Russia and Lithuania, or the Bund. It had taken almost a generation, from 1870 to 1897, for a Jewish socialist party to be born. Among its most militant members were the brush-makers, the tanners and the shop assistants. The work conditions in these three trades were abysmal. The brush-makers' bosses bought pig's bristles at the Leipzig Fair and the workers sorted them and made them into brushes. They worked fourteen hours a day and demanded a reduction to twelve hours and a pay rise. The guild, around a thousand strong, was almost entirely Jewish. The brush-makers were highly respected and Vladimir Medem considered them to be "di smetene" (the cream) of the Bundist movement. The tanners—mostly Jews but also Poles and Lithuanians—worked in the vicinity of Vilnius and Dvinsk (Latvia). They demanded twelve hours a day. Their employers refused and they went on strike for seven weeks.

Finally, there were the shop assistants. Although they were considered a special category, rather like "white collar" workers, and some of them dreamed of opening up their own shops, they worked more than sixteen hours a day for miserable pay.

These three professions, which had rapidly organized themselves into unions, were considered the most intransigent in the Jewish workers' movement. This period, known as "Erev Bund," was the prehistory of the Bund party, and showed how men and women, risking their lives, attacked by the yes-men of the regime, by their employers, by the rabbis, by Russian autocracy, could succeed in galvanizing ardent and proud elements of Jewish youth.

During the first years, the movement's ascension was spectacular. Three thousand strong at its beginning, eight years later, at the 1905 revolution, it had grown to thirty thousand. The struggle was for a democratic, parliamentary regime, for civil and political rights which would lead, as in the West, to the emancipation of the Jews. A democratic organization, the Bund vehemently opposed Bolshevism in October 1917, only to be liquidated three years later. Nevertheless, it lived on in Poland until the Second World War and scored an emphatic victory in the municipal elections at the end of 1938 because it defended impoverished Polish Jews persecuted during the wave of virulent anti-Semitism under the Republic of the Colonels (1935-39).

In 1917, the Balfour declaration triggered the irresistible rise of political Zionism, born at the Basle Congress in 1897. A nationalist and international movement whereas the Bund was national and internationalist, its charismatic leader, Theodor Herzl, declared prophetically, "In fifty years, it will not be a dream but a reality." His words galvanized Yiddishland. During the following years, another wave of youth responded enthusiastically to the call of *Melekh Herzl* (King Herzl). Thousands of young Jews joined the different Zionist movements, from extreme Left to revisionist Right. The last of the nationalist movements in Europe in the 19th century, Zionism, like the Bund, distinguished itself by the tireless militancy of its members.

Zionism recruited its faithful in every strata of Jewish society, but principally in sectors of the working class and middle class. It was fiercely criticized by the Bund and other movements such as the Folkists and autonomist groups, which did not accept Israel as a "gathering together" of the Diaspora. One must note that extreme Zionist factions such as the Marxist-inspired Hashomer Hatzair and Vladimir Jabotinsky's Revisionists, two very dynamic organizations, were poles apart politically. The former, influenced by Russian populism, were partisans of agricultural collectivism. They founded the *kibbutzim* in Palestine. The latter, believers in hierarchy and opposed to unions— the Histadrut—encouraged a leadership cult and preached an authoritarian brand of politics, several of them using Mussolini's Fascism as an example.

The years 1897 and 1917 were crucial. They marked the awakening of the awareness of Judaism, which from then on asserted itself either by taking the road which led to a classless, more just and humane society, or the path to a state for all Jews who wished to make the *alyah* (emigration) to Israel. There were, of course, memorable conflicts between these two ideologies.

Jewish socialist and Zionist organizations were formed in the towns and the *shtetlach*, followed in the 1920s by communist groups. May 1st, Labor Day, was the occasion for impressive demonstrations by Jews and non-Jews united by circumstance in a single struggle. In most towns and villages, three organizations co-existed: the Bund, Poale Zion and the communists. There were therefore often three libraries, three choirs and three theater troupes. In each of the *shtetlach*, local militants worked selflessly, believing in the justness of their chosen creed and inspired by an immense love of humanity and exemplary fraternity. Their role models were their leaders, men like Vladimir Medem or Ber Borokhov, who gave their names to schools, institutions, libraries and study groups.

Other separatist movements sprang up at the beginning of the century. Immediately after the Bolshevik revolution, that "great light in the East," socialists and Zionists joined communist organizations en masse, certain that the new regime heralded a new era of happiness and social justice. The USSR exercised a romantic fascination on the youth of the period, some of whom believed it was a historical necessity. There were ideological and even physical confrontations. And of course there were passionate discussions within families, where the father was a Hasid, the son a Bundist, a Folkist (autonomist), communist, Poale Zionist, Mizrahist or Revisionist.

YIDDISH CULTURE

To be Jewish meant above all to belong to a culture held together by the Yiddish language. André Malraux wrote: "What we call culture is first and foremost the will to recall, to inherit and to enrich what has been noble in the world." Charles Dobzynski gave us the following image: "It is the language of the dispersion and continuity of a people, the language of humble crafts and great sacrifices, of obscure labors and struggles, of obscurantism, misery and oppression. It is the language of the ghetto and of liberty. It articulates the universe and shakes the fences of provincialism in order to become a universal language of poetry drawing its wealth, its fabulous all-pervading conductivity from a permanent fusion of the disparate elements, traditions and inventions which contribute to its metamorphosis. Thus, thanks to the work of Yiddish translators, it has been sown with masterpieces of world literature."

In 1908, seventy delegates from several countries met at the Czernowicz conference in Bukovina, at the eastern extremity of the Austro-Hungarian empire. Some, among them eminent writers, affirmed with bitterness and exaltation that Yiddish was the universal Jewish language, while others considered Hebrew as the only true Jewish tongue. Marked by sectarianism and rowdy debates, the conference at least demonstrated that Yiddish had acquired legitimacy and that it was, if not *the* language, certainly *a* Jewish language. This led to the normalization of Yiddish and the creation of school networks which were in fact the beginning of a linguistic crusade which was to continue for a third of a century, not only in Poland but in all countries where Yiddish was established. Czernowicz also marked the beginning of an effervescence of Yiddish literature hitherto unknown. In less than two generations, Yiddishkeit became the fundamental element of Jewish culture in Yiddishland.

Various literary movements developed modernism's multiple facets. While drawing from tradition, they sublimated the mythical past in order to project into the future. This manifested itself as much by poetic tendencies as by naturalist and social novels. The phenomenon spread beyond the *Alte Heim* (Old Continent) to the *Goldenem Land* (Golden Country) and established itself as far afield as South Africa, South America and Australia.

Yiddish was a vehicle of the epic chants drawn from the immense biblical reservoir, in whose stories and legends the sacred and the fantastic blend harmoniously. From the epic chants, liturgical texts and books of morals came the *mayse* (fables or tales), a genre mastered by Elijah Levita during the Italian Renaissance.

Hasidism also abounds with stories (*aggodoth*) mixing prayers and popular chants glorifying its founder, the *tzaddic* (sage), the just, the spiritual guide, the Ba'al Shem Tov. The remarkable Rabbi Nachman of Bratzlav is the most famous of these storytellers. While the Haskala used Yiddish to enlighten the ignorant and superstitious masses, a modern Yiddish literature with its first popular novels was born.

The three founding fathers of modern Yiddish literature are Mendele Mokher Sefarim, Sholem Aleichem and Isaac Leib Peretz. Mendele wrote about the Jewish villages in the zone of residence with their picaresque and derisory heroes. Sholem Aleichem created quintessentially modern characters, highly symbolic figures in an imaginary world, caught in a process of secularization which announces dramatic events to come. Peretz continued the storytelling tradition as well as excelling in the theater and perfecting the art of the incisive short story.

The period between the two World Wars was the most fertile, despite the often unfavorable political context in several countries. There was exceptional cultural richness and considerable energy, yet at the same time there was a presentiment of the danger and anguish to come. On the steppes of Volhynia, the marshes of the Pripet River, the fertile black soils of the Ukraine, the moors of Pomerelia, in the factories and blast furnaces of Silesia, on the windswept plains of Bessarabia and the lakes of Lithuania, from the skyscrapers of New York to the streets surrounding the Pletzl in Paris, Yiddish writers excelled in all genres: H. Leivick with his Golem, the clay monster invented, it is said, by the Maharal of Prague; Joseph Opatachu with his vivid description of the Polish forests; David Edelstadt, Morris Rosenfeld and Morris Vinchevsky, the proletarian poets and transatlantic bards of the sweatshops; poets Mani-Leib, Glanz Leyeles and, closer to home, Avrom Reizen, Eliezer Steinbarg; the novelist Moshe Kulbak, the disillusioned creator of the Zelminien family; the family sagas of Soviet writer and poet, David Bergelson; the *Musarnikes*, the Talmudic students who took refuge in asceticism, of the Litvak Haim Grade; Avrom Sutzkever, the magician of word and rhyme and passionate lover of Vilnius; Smerke Kaczerginski, the poet of the Shoah and the resistance; the frenetic vitality of Peretz Markich; the terror of extermination of Itzhak Katzenelson; the flamboyant humor of Itsik Manger; Sholem Asch, one of the rare writers to live from his work and who brought the fascinating cities of St. Petersburg, Warsaw and Moscow to life; and of course Isaac Bashevis Singer.

Many of them met tragic ends. And inevitably, sadly, the list is incomplete. To compile a critical survey of Yiddish literature is almost impossible. All is upheaval, a jumble of exterior influences (Rilke, Pushkin, Verlaine, Zola, Maupassant) and genres (realism, naturalism, romanticism, futurism, expressionism). Yiddish literature spans more than a hundred years, from the French Revolution to the Treaty of Versailles and then a period between the wars which was full of hope but which saw the inexorable escalation of the perils which culminated in the Shoah. It spanned places (Poland, the Soviet Union, the United States). And, at the same time, there was the growing competition of the Hebrew language, whose triumph came with the foundation of the state of Israel.

Yiddishland can be characterized by its humor, by its way of translating the trials of life into laughter. Laughter is the antidote to fatality, to an often hostile environment, and is a derivative of difficult times. Often drawn from holy texts or from literature, Jewish humor is never coarse or vulgar. Even derision can express optimism and hope.

Yiddish humor is built on a solid literary tradition derived from the Hasidic tales and above all the Yiddish writers already mentioned, such as Mendele, whose *Fishke the Lame* and *The Journey of Benjamin III* are full of comical and absurd situations, and Sholem Aleichem, with his *Tevye the Milkman* and *Railway Tales*. A number of their works have entered the theatrical comedy repertoire. Sholem Aleichem, who lived in America at the end of his life, coined many

Jewish American or Yinglish terms in his humorous writings. And, of course, there are the fables of Moshe Nadir and Itsik Manger, *A Story in Paradise*.

Yiddishland humor can be facetious. A *witz* is a joke, a *mayse* is a story and a *klole* is a curse. Leo Rosten compiled a famous anthology of Jewish jokes (*The Joys of Yiddish*). Woody Allen often tells them in his movies. In fact, American Jewish humor, often in Yinglish, has always been present in transatlantic movies, from Harold Lloyd and the Marx Brothers down to Mel Brooks. In France, Itzhok Opatowski wrote a short book, *Lomir lachen* (Let's Laugh), translated into French under the title *Rire et sourire*, followed recently by *Jewish Humour* by Joseph Klatzmann.

There is a great variety of Yiddish proverbs. They are a treasury of wisdom and common sense, often bitter-sweet, sometimes sad, always expressing the vitality and the humanity of a people whose sense of humor dates back to the Bible. And finally there are the curses, generally originating from Vilnius, and which Alain Spiraux made a specialty of.

Clearly, the particular Yiddish savor, the *taam*, is often lost in translation. We know that minority communities have their own cultural defense reflexes which preserve their originality and cultural specificity. It is a sign of vitality and *joie de vivre* in the face of a precarious existence, poverty and life's torments. A phrase keeps coming back: "Abi gezunt." Let's hope our health lasts.

The Yiddish press had an unusual development. In Poland, there were thirty daily newspapers between the wars. The two largest, *Haynt* (Today) and *Moment*, published in Warsaw, had circulations of almost one hundred thousand each. The periodicals and weekly magazines, twice-monthly and monthly reviews and satirical newspapers reflected not only the wide spectrum of Jewish political opinion but also the literary, artistic, medical and professional worlds. There were two illustrated publications for children, one of which, *Grininke Baymelekh* (Little Green Trees), was a classic of the genre. The principal New York paper, *Forverts* (Forward), from 1910 to 1930 had a daily circulation of more than two hundred and fifty thousand. Its talented and authoritarian editor, Abe Cahan, a self-taught man, gave the paper a resolute modernity equal to the great American dailies in English. There were also, of course, Hebrew, Polish and other national language newspapers, but Yiddish predominated. From the birth of the Yiddish press in 1686 until today, it is estimated there have been more than three thousand different publications.

The Jewish theater, which had existed for more than a century, owed its development to the Vilne Trupe, the Yung-Teater, the Varshever Yiddisher Kunst-Teater (Warsaw Theater of Yiddish Art) with Zygmunt Turkov and Ida Kaminski, and the Habima (Hebrew Theater) which grew up in Israel. The themes of the dramas were drawn from Jewish literature, folk tradition and non-Jewish classical and contemporary writers. *Der Dybbuk* by S. Ansky and Shakespeare's plays were enormously popular. In the 1930s, in Poland alone, there were thirty theater troupes. And one must not forget Yiddish cinema, which reached its height before the Second World War.

Primary and secondary schools proliferated everywhere in Yiddishland. The backbone of the system were the *Hadorim, Talmudei Torah* and *yeshivot* but, due to social developments, the religious authorities created the reformed *heder*. The Agoudat was a dense network of religious schools. The orthodox Zionist Mizrahi created their own *Yavne* schools. At the same time, secular Yiddish education flourished with the ZISHO school network, comprised of the Yiddish secular schools and the dominantly Hebrew-speaking *Tarbut* (culture) schools. Both were full time, mixed, employed pedagogy considerably ahead of its time and attracted more than sixty thousand Jewish children annually. These school networks can be accredited to modernist Judaism. They ensured the maintenance of Jewish identity and an acute national consciousness. Complementary courses (*Tsugabshul*), technical colleges (ORT) and youth movements of various creeds consolidated this institutional fabric.

University education and teaching was enriched by the creation of several institutes in the Soviet Union and Poland. The YIVO in Vilnius was famous for its prestigious staff of researchers, sociologists, historians and linguists. Simon Dubnov observed that the "creation in one year in the Jerusalem of Palestine and in the Jerusalem of Lithuania of two similar institutions was not a coincidence but a symbolic act."

TODAY AND TOMORROW

Those who survived remember with emotion and nostalgia their lost youth. They were the miserable and filthy children of those towns and villages, plump in appearance but who in reality lived hard times in an often hostile world.

Imagine those Jews with their clothes and trappings. Roam the streets from Piotrkowska to Lodz, Gesia to Warsaw, or from Zavalna to Vilnius. The small furriers', rag merchants' and cobblers' shops and the delicious-smelling bakeries are all gone. Gone are the people, the *oylem*, the bourgeois in his sombre frock coat, starched collar and top hat, the workers with their peaked caps and their tunics, the students of the *yeshivot* with their traditional caftans, *shtraymels* (fur hats), their beards and *peyes* (curls) blowing in the wind, the women wearing the *shaitel* (wig) and the children in rags or navy blue suits. Like a painful litany, one must go on repeating that these rabbis, teachers, schoolchildren, shopkeepers, craftsmen, manual workers, community leaders and politicians have all disappeared. Those streets are empty now and if you visit the old Jewish towns in Europe, particularly in Poland, you need a lot of imagination to picture them as they were before. The Jews are no longer part of the landscape.

We must remember the *frumakes* (pious Jews) and the "fraye denker" (free thinkers). We must also remember the words of Elie Wiesel: "One can be for or against God but not without Him." And we must question ourselves about His silence during the horror and abomination of fifty years ago.

Yiddishland disappeared with the Shoah. Even if a few centers still survive here and there, even if there has been a certain renaissance, it has only been a transient one. "We have definitely lost eastern Europe, and we still have not understood the gravity of this," wrote Alexandre Adler. Yiddishland never recovered from genocide. In Europe, two-thirds of its population had their lives brutally taken away from them. But one must be in no haste to chant the Requiem or recite the Kaddish. A new form of Yiddishkeit continues through translations and with the "generation afterward". The Jewish people have always been fragile and vulnerable but, curiously, it is precisely this which has ensured their survival. If the Shoah was the tragic end of the lost world of Yiddishland, its spirit undoubtedly lives on in Judaism and, beyond the boundaries of Yiddishland, in the non-Jewish world. Every trauma, every crisis, no matter how dramatic, implies continuity and a future under other skies and in other latitudes. To quote *A Thousand Years of Ashkenazi Culture*: "Even nostalgia and our longing for the lost is in fact the present, the here and now, the road into the future." And the poem of Jacob Glatstein:

Only a voice
disembodied words

carriers
of that which is never effaced
spun in your memory
listen to your voice
joy woven with nostalgia and absence
wreath of flames
nostalgia—absence of roots
and their joy of their joy.

These photographs, postcards, faces and landscapes are invaluable to us. They allow us to relive the past, they incite us to remember. They are a paper monument waiting to be rediscovered. The antidote to forgetting is memory. "There is never enough time to recover a memory," said Edmond Jabes. As for Ba'al Shem Tov, he declared: "Memory is the root of deliverance, like forgetting is that of exile." The world of Yiddishland is now history, legend, and will remain so forever. Am Israel khaï.

THE POSTCARD, YIDDISHLAND'S MEMORY

On October 1st, 1869, a plain, unillustrated card measuring nine by fourteen centimeters, the invention of an Austrian Jew, Doctor Emmanuel Hermann, a teacher at the Academy of Commerce in Graz, was officially approved by the postal administration of the Austro-Hungarian empire. The postcard was born.

Immediately sensing the extraordinary development this administrative innovation was to have, publishers sent photographers to the remotest districts to record for posterity the curious local customs and activities of their inhabitants. Hundreds of thousands of postcards rapidly reached the most out-of-the-way places, bringing to their addressees images of worlds hitherto undreamed of.

For several years now, researchers from many disciplines—historians, sociologists, archivists and architects—have drawn increasingly frequently on these testimonies of the popular imagery of our time. The postcard was the subject of a ten-line entry in the *Grande Encyclopédie* of 1885. A forty-page study, copiously illustrated, was devoted to it in the 1989 *Encyclopedia Judaica*, whose publisher rightly considered that it would become a fundamental vehicle of Jewish collective memory.

Although Yiddishland had disappeared by the end of the Second World War, it lives on thanks to the millions of postcards found in attics and family archives or sold during publishers' stock clearances or liquidations.

Despite their frozen imagery, these small cards faithfully re-create the immutable rhythms of the *shtetl*, and relate in great detail the humble trades which prevented entire poverty-stricken populations from dying of hunger.

Through them, the bushy-bearded rabbis, professional marriage brokers, itinerant water carriers, bright-eyed *yeshivot* students, porters and peddlers, workers wearing their traditional flat caps and the bourgeois Jews who were integrated into Russian society all live on.

They record for eternity the villages devastated by the Tsar's Black Hundreds. Cards showing corpses of children wrapped in their *tallithim* were sent to members of the French parliament so that they could comprehend the extent of the pogroms and exert their influence to bring them to an end.

They reveal the architecture of the wooden synagogues, from the humblest to the most sumptuous, burnt one after the other, as were entire Jewish towns during the weeks following the lightning advance of Hitler's forces into the Soviet Union.

In short, these documents, frozen moments in the passage of time, render possible an overall picture of a civilization which might otherwise have been forgotten.

But who were their publishers, and in which countries were they established? And what motivated them—a desire to serve Jewish communities or commercial expediency? No doubt both.

Yehudia, Central, Libanon, Synaj and Resnik in Warsaw, Phoenix in Berlin and Hebrew Publishing and Williamsburg in New York were all exclusively dedicated to publishing Jewish postcards. Some of their non-specialized competitors, particularly in Poland and in Germany, also invested in this niche market.

Cards illustrating the everyday events of the *shtetl*—circumcisions, Bar Mitzvahs, marriages, funerals and the events of the Hebraic calendar—were posted by millions of Jews to one another, sometimes written in Hebrew, but usually in Yiddish or the language of the country in which they were resident.

Surprisingly, the most true-to-life pictures of the "Jewish street" were taken by the roving German army war photographers between 1914 and 1918, only a few of whom signed their work. A series of cards carry the credit "A. Kuhlewind, official war photographer", whose "original photographs" were published by the Hochland brothers in Konigsberg. Another card states that the "original photograph" was "taken on campaign by non-commissioned officer Boedecker of the 12th Infantry Regiment" and produced by 'Boedecker, Publishers, Berlin'. Soldier Boedecker supplemented his wages by publishing his military work.

Of course, civilian production of postcards continued throughout the war and there are many cards illustrating Yiddishland that carry the publisher's name and origin. For the Berlin-based German Bookshop and Publishers for Universal Knowledge, Hister in London and Dutton in New York (who printed in Bavaria) business went on as usual. Louis Lamm in Berlin even specialized in "Jewish war postcards".

Several organizations, including Munich Aid to Eastern Prussia, the Association of Bavarian War Comrades and the German and Russian Red Cross, donated the proceeds from their card sales to war victim support.

But the majority of publishing was done directly by the military authorities with the "authorization of the Interior Ministry" of each of the German empire's various dominions. Publications produced by campaign headquarters, by "Group 1 of the 10th Division in Russian Poland", by the "Campaign Bookshops" of the forces stationed in Kiev, and by the Bug and Baranovichi divisions were printed in Vienna and Leipzig and "distributed behind the front line". In this way the army often took the place of peace-time publishers, providing the soldiers with postcards that reflected their everyday experiences in the field.

In certain regiments, blank cards with "army post correspondence" printed on one side were distributed, intended for soldiers wishing to sketch scenes that caught their eye. The best of them were then published in limited editions. Most of them were caricatures, whose exaggerated features reveal a visceral rather than doctrinal anti-Semitism. When, in 1964, for family reasons, I became interested in Judaic postcards, I was stupefied by the abundance and wealth of my discoveries. I was immediately swept into an exploration which was as exhausting as it was exalting. Tirelessly, magnifying glass in hand, I rummaged through the bookstalls on the banks of the Seine, dusty bookshops, the Parisian flea markets, suburban junk sales and specialist salons. The mineral I extracted from these mines which I systematically exploited vein by vein resulted in a collection of several tens of thousands of Jewish postcards.

Yiddishland's heartland is shown in grey
(18—20th century)

VILNA

On September 18th, 1915, Yom Kippur, Vilnius
fell to the Germans. In 1916, they organized
an "Exhibition of the workshops of Vilnius".
The advertisement is in four languages, including
Yiddish. Vilnius, Vilna, Wilna and Wilno have all been
official names of the town during its chequered history.

40

Das Geschäftsviertel der Juden in Wilna

The Jewish shopping district.

Der Krieg im Osten
Wilna
In der Judengasse

41

Jatrowa Street in the Jewish quarter.

Wilna   Hof im
Judenviertel

42

Zu den Juden-Verfolgungen in Wilna.
Blick in die Fleischmarktgasse, dem alten Ghetto der Juden, nach der Einnahme durch die Polen.

"Vilnius's persecuted Jews after the town's fall to the Poles: a view of the meat market in the old ghetto." The caption by a German war correspondent gives the reason why the Jewish population welcomed the Kaiser's troops as liberators.
Opposite: a typical courtyard in the Jewish quarter.

44

WILNA — Wilno. Gettho izraelicka — DAS JÜDISCHE GHETTO

A street in the Jewish quarter.

WILNA. Alte jüdische Straße

The entrance to the *shulhoyf*, the courtyard of the synagogue. The synagogue of Gaon in Vilnius, built in 1800, is visible beyond the gate in the background. The Strashun library is on the right.

Der Krieg im Osten   Wilna — Lebhafter Handel vor dem Flickerladen

46

The Jewish quarter's many humble trades: second-hand clothes and shoe sellers,
religious booksellers, tinsmiths, water carriers and workhands.
In the market, Jewish women are recognizable by their chequered shawls.

48

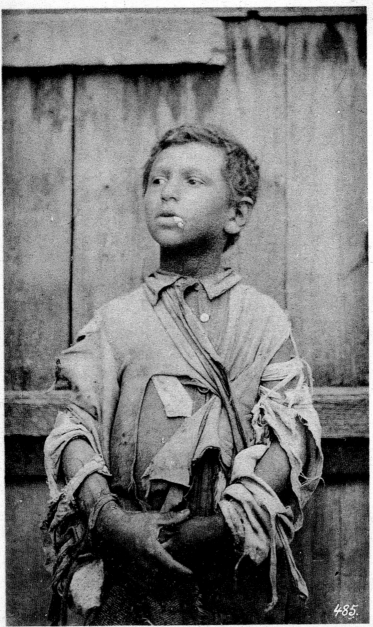

Vom östlichen Kriegsschauplatz. Jüdischer Bettelknabe

Der Krieg im Osten
Wilna — Im Judenviertel

49

Children in the Jewish quarter.
Opposite: a Jewish beggar.

Der Krieg im Osten
Wilna — Im Judenviertel

50

Life in the Jewish quarter.

צייטונגס-קיאסק
„די יודישע וועלט"
Soldatenführer durch Wilna
РУССКIЙ В
לעצטע נייס
Deutsche Tageszeitung
ZEITUNG
HANDLUNG

52

53

Life in the Jewish quarter.
Opposite: a news stand with a sign in Yiddish on the roof indicating that the German army newspaper is sold. Another sign underneath says the kiosk sells Yiddish newspapers from all over the world.

54

Jüd. Buchhändler

Booksellers.
Opposite: a Jew and a Lithuanian gentile selling the German army newspaper in Vilnius.
Following pages: Jewish shops and workshops.

Zeitungsverkäufer

WILNA. Judenviertel

Water carriers in the Jewish quarter.

Workhands waiting to be hired.
Following pages: street musicians singing and playing popular melodies on the barrel organ, a trade practiced by both men and women.

62

Vom östlichen Kriegsschauplatz Wilnaer Hofmusikanten

63

Jüdische Hof-Musikanten

64

מרדכי צבי מאַנע   מיכה יוסף לבנזון

Left: Micah Joseph Lebensohn (Vilnius, 1828-1852), considered the greatest of the poets of the Haskala.
Right: Mordecir Zevi Manne, born in Vilnius in 1859. This poet and painter was inspired
particularly by religious themes and the history of the Jewish people.
Opposite: Judah Leib Gordon, a poet who wrote in Hebrew, born in Vilnius in 1831.
Initially a denigrator of Yiddish, he later published *Sihat Hullin*, a collection of poems in the language.

יהודה ליב גארדאן

66

WILNO. Synagoga   Fot. J. Bułhak

Wilna. Die alte Jüdische Synagoge

The synagogue and entrance to the Strashun library, built in 1901.
Opposite: the entrance to the Gaon synagogue in Vilnius.

68

Wilna   Judentypen

Selling religious books.

TYPY WILNA. PRZY TALMUDZIE.

69

Talmudists in the old synagogue.

The Jewish cemetery in Vilnius.
Opposite: *klogerin*, professional mourners, in front of a tomb in the cemetery in Vilnius. They were hired for the seven days of mourning stipulated by Jewish law for the month of Elul, during which tombs are traditionally visited. Wailing loudly, they chanted improvised prayers in Yiddish.

72

The dining room of an orphanage.
Following pages: a laic summer camp in the 1930s.

9.VIII.1933 /ק־80 תרצ״ג

LODZ

Jews and Poles on the first barricades in June 1905,
fighting side by side against the Tsarist regime.
The savage repression after the uprising resulted
in hundreds of dead and wounded.

Łódź, Widok ogólny.
Lodz, Total-Ansicht.

In 1910, the city's total population of 410,000 included 167,000 Jews.

80

ŁÓDŹ. Dzielnica północno-wschodnia

Lodz was known as "the Polish Manchester": in 1914 there were 175 mills and factories, a third of them Jewish owned.
Opposite: the factory of the textile magnate, Itzhok K. Poznanski, where 6,300 employees worked.
A menial mill worker who climbed to the very top of the social ladder, he built the sumptuous
Poznanski Palace for himself in Lodz.

Łódź   Fabryka Tow. Akc. I. K. Poznański

81

ŁÓDŹ. Pałac Poznańskiego — Le palais Poznański.

The "Jewish street", with its characteristic trades and characters.

Łódź   Ulica Piotrkowska

Piotrkowska Street, in the town center. Jews, recognizable by their traditional costume (flat cap and long black coat buttoned on the left), go about their business. In 1914, a quarter of the town's 20,000 stalls and shops were Jewish owned.

Szpital Żydowski.   Jüdisches Hospital.   No. 10.

84

Łódz, „Talmud-Tora".

"To be in good health is to be already rich" (a Yiddish proverb).
The Talmud Torah, founded in 1873 by Elijah Hayyim Meisel.

Kondukt żałobny rabina Majzla w Łodzi.

85

The funeral of Rabbi Meisel in 1912. Renowned for his philanthropy, he built a mill to employ workers made redundant by the mechanization of the textile industry.

Fot. B. Wilkoszewski, Łódź

Naśladownictwo Zastrzeżone.

Vieille Sinagoge à Lodź.

Лодзь
,Синагога'
Łódź
Synagoga
Synagoge à
rue
Spacerowa.

Jüdischer Kirchhof mit russischen Schützengräben bei Lodz

Above, opposite and following pages: the number and size of the synagogues in Lodz were proof of the city's intense religious life. They were all destroyed by the Nazis in 1939.

88

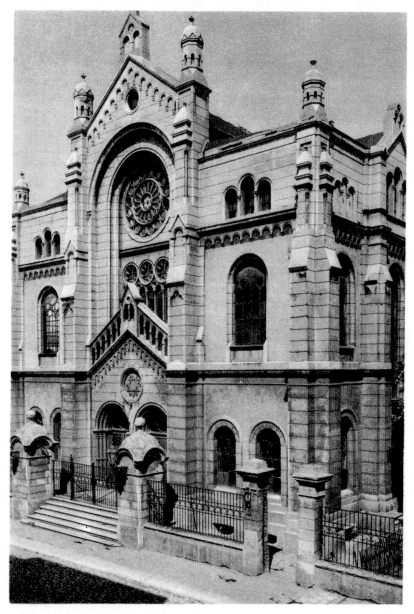

ŁÓDŹ Synagoga przy ul. Wólczańskiej.
Synagogue, Rue Wólczańska.

Łódź   Wewnątrz Synagogi, przy uł. Spacerowej
Lodz   Inneres der Synagoge an der Promenadenstraße

Łódź. Typy z bruku łódzkiego.
Lodz. Lodzer Typen.

Morning prayer (Shaharit). The man on the left wears on his forehead the small leather box containing the Shema (the prayer Jews must recite twice a day): "Hear o Israel".
Opposite: returning from the synagogue, the man on the left with his *tallit* (prayer shawl) under his arm, the other wearing his shtreimel, the traditional fur hat.

Typy z Królestwa Polskiego.
Typen aus Russisch Polen.

92

Leopold Pilichowski, born in 1869 a few kilometers from Lodz,
was particularly fond of painting the textile workers of the Jewish Manchester.
The great storyteller David Frischmann, born in 1859 in Zgierz, lived and
worked in Lodz where, in 1909, he published four volumes of his writings in Yiddish.

VERLAG URIEL.

93

In 1918, the first Yiddish school was named after Ber
Borokhov, founder and theorist of socialist Zionism (Poale Zion).
Born in Belorussia in 1886, Itzhak Katzenelson, author of the
Yiddish poem, *The Song of the Assassinated Jewish People*, moved
to Lodz where he opened a Hebraic secondary school which
he directed until the outbreak of the Second World War.

94

Łódź. Typy Łódzkie ~ Lodz. Lodzer Typen

Lottery ticket sellers.

Łódź. Typy z bruku łódzkiego.
Lodz. Typen von Lodz.

"**N**o matter how menial, a trade is a trade" (Yiddish proverb).

Łódź: Typy z bruku łódzkiego.
Lodz: Lodzer Typen.

Lodsch, Aus dem Judenviertel (Baluty)

When the German army entered Lodz, on September 8th, 1939, war correspondents resorted to the same clichés their predecessors had used in 1914. **O**pposite: workhands waited for work in all the commercial quarters.

"**W**ithout manual labor there can be no science" (Yiddish proverb).
Opposite: "A carpenter without his tools is not a carpenter" (Yiddish proverb).

Lodz. Targ, stary rynek – Markt, alter Ring.

"Commerce is not the practice of fraternity" (Yiddish proverb).

101

Vom Markt in Lodz

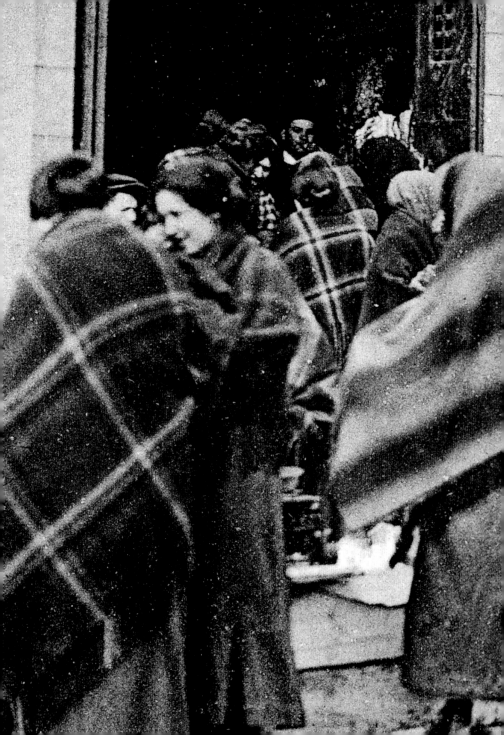

Vor der Fleischhalle in Lodz

Jewish women buying fish the day before Shabbat.

„פֿאָלקס-ליעדער."

מיין קינד, מיין טריסט, דו פֿאָהרסט-אװעק,
זעה, די א זון א נומער,
דיך בעט מיט טרעהרען און מיט שרעק
דיין טריע ליעבע מוטער.
דו פֿאָהרסט, מיין קינד, מיין איינצינ קינד,—
איבער װיטע ימען,
אך קום אהין נור פֿריש, געזונד
און נישט פֿערגעס דיין מאמען:

א פֿריװאלע דער מאמען.

H. GOLDBERG

Originalaufnahme vom Kriegsschauplatz 1915
Deutscher Landwehrmann im Gespräch mit Juden in Lodz

105

"Clients can be found for everything except worries" (Yiddish proverb).
Opposite: between the wars, hundreds of thousands of eastern European Jews emigrated all over the world.

"People's faces depend on the eyes they are seen with" (Yiddish proverb).

Group photographs taken in 1915 immediately after the Germans' arrival in Lodz, to be cut up into individual portraits by the occupying authorities and attached to compulsory identity cards.

Łódź podczas wojny 1914/15. Tania kuchnia żydowska.
Lodz während des Krieges 1914/15. Vor der jüdischen billigen Küche.

Poverty grew during the first months of the war, after the Kaiser's troops
occupied Lodz. Soup kitchens were opened, some serving kosher food for the Jews.

A special Yiddish edition of the German army newspaper was
published and distributed by the troops to the Jewish population in Lodz.

Straßenleben in Lodz
nach der Einnahme durch die Deutschen.

7253
Verlag von
GUSTAV LIERSCH & Cᵒ.
BERLIN S.W.

The German army, heavily present in the city, showing no hostility to the Jews.

GEMEINSCHAFT DEUTSCHER SAMMLER e.V. · GAU WARTHELAND · KAMERADSCHAFT DER BRIEFMARKENFREUNDE LITZMANNSTADT

1. POSTWERTZEICHENSCHAU

13.—16. JUNI 1942

LITZMANNSTADT

Litzmannstadt, Adolf-Hitler-Strasse — rechts Fremdenhof „Gen. Litzmann"

At the end of October 1939, Piotrkowska Street, Lodz's main
artery, became Adolf Hitler Street. The Jews disappeared overnight.
Opposite: in early December 1939, Lódz was annexed by the Reich and renamed Litzmannstadt.
Following pages: on February 8th, 1940, the German administration officially created
a ghetto with the Balut quarter as its center. On April 30th it was cordoned off with
160,000 Jews enclosed within. In September, 1944, every Jew in Lodz was exterminated.

THE STREET

Typical Jews from around Myslovice,
a town sixty kilometers west of Kraków.

118

Паровой Кожевенный Заводъ Х. Фрейнкеля, Шавли.

Siauliai (Shavli in Yiddish), a town in northern Lithuania, whose population was three-quarters Jewish. The Hayyim Frenki tannery, founded in 1880, was an early example of the formidable vitality of Jewish entrepreneurs who would later own most of the chemical and steel industries.

Goduzischki.

The village of Adustiskis in Lithuania, approximately 100 kilometers from Vilnius.
Liepaja (Lebanon) in Latvia, whose Jewish population arrived en masse from the provinces at
the end of the 19th century, drawn there by the Baltic port's advantageous geographic position.

Der Krieg
im Osten
Brüder Schmul

Stimmungsbild in einer Straße
in Schaulen (Szawle)

War and exodus. Jews under the protection of the "pointed helmets".
Opposite: the Schmul children, brothers in poverty.
Following pages: a busy market in Minsk, capital of Belorussia.
Before the First World War, half its population was Jewish.

Judenmarkt in Minsk

124

Deutsche Truppen auf der Rast
in dem von uns besetzten Lida (Rußland).

The Jews of Lia in eastern Poland going peacefully about their business among the soldiers' stacked arms. Today Lia is located in Belorussia.

Sionim, a three-quarters Jewish town, was devastated by the war. Cholera decimated
the poor, who were undernourished and lived in miserable, unhealthy conditions.

126

Watched benevolently by the Kaiser's troops,
the very poorest queue in front of a Jewish soup kitchen.

In Brest Litovsk (Brisk in Yiddish) Jewish businesses were closed after the expulsions
carried out first by the Russians then by the Germans during the summer of 1915.
Opposite: a familiar silhouette in Piaski's main square.

Hauptstrasse von Piaski

129

IWANOWO - Eine Judengasse.

130

Nowogrodek
Jüdischestraße

Fragile dwellings which were all burned down, either by
the Tsar's Black Hundreds or by the Einsatzgruppen of the SS.
At the turn of the century, this small town was 60% Jewish.

Nowaja Mysch
Judenstraße

Wooden houses on the Jewish street in the small country town of Novaya Mysh.

Small shops and stalls, where people gathered to meet and chat, were the main commercial organs, both in large towns such as Pinsk or in the country.

Strasse in Pinsk.

134

Die Straße in Wolkowysk.

A group of Jewish women in Pinsk, recognizable by their large shawls.
Following pages: Jewish women washing in a river. In other European countries, Jews were
forbidden to wash in rivers where Christians bathed, because, it was said, of the risk of pollution.

17 Stawiski. Juden am Brunnen.

In einer polnischen Judenstadt

Im Judenviertel in Sosnowicze.

Posing face to face: a German soldier and a group of Jews at the entrance to a *shtetl* (a Jewish village).
The Jewish quarter of Sosnowiec, which had a population of around three thousand Jews at the end of the last century.
Opposite: Jews at a well in the Polish town of Stawiski.

A wealthy Jewish house in the town of Biala.
Houses in this province often had outside staircases and landings.
Opposite: in certain respects, Kraków's Polish architecture resembles that of Vilnius in Lithuania.

142

A rabbi and a beggar pose voluntarily next to an Austrian soldier with a bayonet attached to the muzzle of his rifle.
Opposite: in the old quarter of Leszno, Jews and Polish peasants apparently living in perfect harmony.

143

Alt-Lissa

Foto. Aufnahme u. Verlag von Samuś Breslauer, Lissa i. P.

144

Zyrardow, 2o.11o

L. Schw. Meinen Brief-noch vor den Feierta-
gen geschrieben mit Coup. für Hertha hoffe rich-
tig in deinen Händen. Antwort von Merkur habe bis
jetzt nicht erhalten und urgire ich darum. Hoffe
dich wolauf. Brief vermutl. verloren gegangen. Gruss

Public transport in Zyrardow, a town with a population of two and a half thousand,
forty-five kilometers from Warsaw. The name of this *shtetl* comes from that of the French
industrialist, Philippe de Gérard, who built textile mills there in the 19th century.

Warszawa
Omnibus z prowincji

145

The irony of the postcard's caption is obvious.
This "provincial omnibus" was far from ideal for transporting passengers or goods.

A railway station platform somewhere in Poland.

148

After the Second World War, there were no survivors from the Jewish community
in the town of Osweicim in Poland, three thousand-strong before the First World War.
The town of Oswiecim became tragically famous under its germanized name of Auschwitz.

Kielce
Ulica Duża

The Jews of the town of Kielce suffered the unthinkable: a pogrom hardly a year after their liberation from the concentration camps. Around two hundred survivors of the genocide were attacked by Polish nationalists and communists united in their anti-Semitism.Officially, there were forty-two dead and dozens of injured.

150

A bustling Jewish street.
Polish peasants in a Jewish area.

Puławy — Ul. Lubelska

151

Juden in Rava.

Puławy (Pilev in Yiddish) was three-quarters Jewish.
Shabbat, day of rest.

152

In most urban areas, the Jewish quarter was confined to the outside of town.
In Lublin, it was along the banks of a river which carried the town's sewage.

153

A smiling man, "posing" complacently in the Jewish quarter of Lublin.

Typische Einwohner von Neu-Sandec beschauen sich eine vorbeiziehende deutsche Wache.

Phot. R. Sennecke.

The population watch with satisfaction as German soldiers who liberated them from the Tsarist yoke march past.

On the eve of the First World War, Ostrolera was Jewish. During the war, the town was bombarded and violent fighting left only ruins and desolation.

Zensiert
Paul Hoffmann & Co.
Berlin-Schöneberg.

Geschäfts-Strasse in dem eroberten Bialystock.

156

Unsere Feldgrauen im Verkehr mit der jüdischen Bevölkerung Russ. Polens.

A German officer outside a cobbler's shop in Bialystok, after it was taken from the Russians.
The Kaiser's troops were popular with the Jews.

Straße in Biala

157

War photographers constantly played on the good
relations between the occupying troops and the Jewish population.

158

A military band playing for the inhabitants of the Jewish quarter, with Jewish children holding their music for them.

„POLNISCHE TYPEN"

160

736. RUSSISCHE TYPEN - Markt.

Taken in 1915, this picture shows a man and his daughter not under arrest but under German protection.
A Russian officer in a market before the German occupation.

Jews and German soldiers fraternizing in Kurow.

11

A provincial scene.

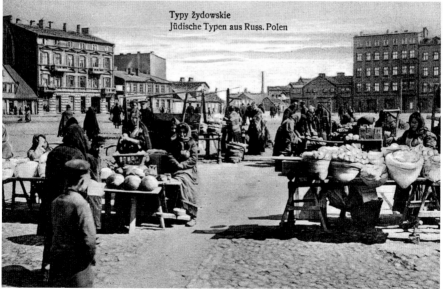

Typy żydowskie
Jüdische Typen aus Russ. Polen

Traditionalists and modernists side by side, dressed differently and both bearded and shaven.
A small district market in a large town.

Mlawa
Jüdische Verkäuferinnen

The provincial market of Mlawa was so famous that
inhabitants of Warsaw went there by train to do their shopping.

Polish peasant men and women selling produce on makeshift stalls.

A French traveler, who lost his way in this village of some five hundred inhabitants, visited the market and photographed this group of Jewish children surrounded by Polish peasants.

NOWY-DWÒR. RYNEK. (Marché)
Dobry - Ładny !... Très joli !...

168

Rzeszów. Rynek — Ringplatz.

A typical market in a *shtetl*, where Jews were the majority just before the First World War.
Long black silhouettes, a statue, a few trees, a provincial square...a lost world.
Opposite: "a typical local man" enjoying a pinch of snuff.

Lemberg 22/5-08

Types du pays.

Firma: Wolf Hirsch et Schlamasel.

Przedruk wzbroniony.

Contrary to the Christian idea, begging bestowed a certain dignity on those who exercised this "menial trade" and the "schnorrer" was not considered a social parasite. Opposite: the bosses of the firm of Wolf Hirsch and Schlamazel.

172

Warsaw, Varche in Yiddish, capital of Poland, had a population of around
three hundred and fifty thousand Jews, whose effervescence gave rise to a highly
organized network of political, cultural and religious institutions and trade unions.
Opposite: Jews and Poles, differing only by their beards and hats.
Following pages: Jewish beggars in Poland.

Typen aus Russ.—Polen.
Jude u. Pole.

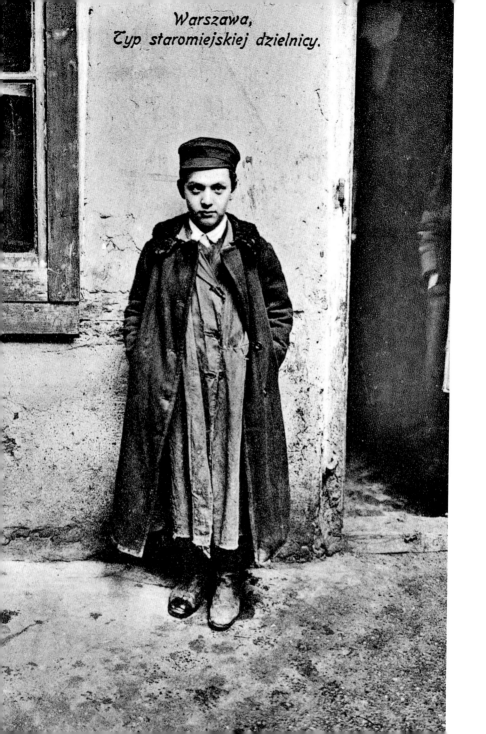

Warszawa,
Typ staromiejskiej dzielnicy.

Schmiel Aron w Sokołowie

Jews in Stawiski.
The Jewish butchers' guild in Stawiski.
Opposite: the card's caption, "Polish Jews", leads us to believe all Jews wear Hasidic dress.

Chère Soeur. — Ne m'écriver plus ici car dans une semaine je retourne en Suisse. — Je ne peux pas vous le dire combien je regrette de quitter ma famille. — Mais, enfin ces quelques semaines de joie m'ont fait beaucoup de bien. — Merci bien pour les nouvelles. —

Les juifs Polonais.

Mille baisers, mes meilleurs amitiés Thayla L. —

Lakepene '4 05

Przedruk wzbroniony. 1904.

Polnische
Judentypen
809

A Jewish family.
Opposite: a beggar in Balut, a working class district of Lodz. This photograph
was used by Nazi propagandists as an illustration of the Litzmannstadt ghetto.

Jews in Pinsk, with ruins in the background.

A pupil at the *heder* (Jewish elementary school for 3 to 13-year-olds),
holding his Siddur (book of prayers for the year).

Makow Podhalanski. In this village of less than two hundred inhabitants, the photographer has caught a young man in modern dress, possibly a student from nearby Kraków, whom one would not expect to find in these surroundings.

A traditional Yiddishland scene. The dress and the handwritten correspondence reinforce the authenticity.
Opposite: after school, a quick smoke before Shabbat.

הוצאת „פלא‎". „בעלי בתים‎" קטנים.

Panje! Kleba?

A young Jewish boy and two Polish peasant girls somewhere in the country.

Racionz bei Mława.   Judentypen

Jews in Raclaz hemmed in by soldiers.

Juden-Typen aus Racionz bei Mlawa   (Russ.-Polen).

German soldiers watching behind posing Jews.
Following pages: in 1914, the famous journalist and humorist, Sandor Friedrich Rosenfeld,
better known as Roda Roda, was sent to write a report somewhere in Austrian Galicia.

An entirely Jewish *shtetl*, probably in Austrian Galicia.

Ein Findling des Roten Kreuzes.
Ein im Ghetto von Warschau aufgefundenes Waisenkind
wird unter grosser Freude der Einwohner vom Roten Kreuz
in Pflege genommen.

Kr. 258 b
Verlag von
Gustav Liersch & Co.,
Berlin

R. Sennecke
phot.

"**A** baby abandoned in the ghetto and, to the great joy of the inhabitants, cared for by the Red Cross".

196

On the road to Lvov, a neighboring large town. Czernowicz is only a few kilometers from the small town of Sadagora. Faithful from all over the province traveled to Sadagora to consult Moshe David Friedman, the miraculous Hasidic rabbi whose fame spread beyond the frontiers of the Ukraine to surrounding lands.

TYPY ŽIDOVSKÝCH FIAKRISTŮ Z HUSTU
NAKL. I. REIZA KNIHKUPEC HUST PODK. RUS:

Khust, high in the Carpathian Mountains where, due to the climate, fur jackets were worn instead of the traditional kaftan.

375

Jüdin aus Druszkopol

The *shtetl* of Kamien Koszyiski.
Opposite: a young Jewish woman in Duzhapol.

200

Gruss aus Eydtkuhnen Ostpr.
Synagogenstrasse

The bourgeoisie of Chernyshevskoye photographed in the street of the synagogue.
Opposite: a street in the ghetto of the small town of Kovel, half the population of which was Jewish.

Judengasse, Kowel.

Fifteen thousand Jews lived in this Ukrainian conglomeration at the beginning of the First World War.

Shops and Jewish passers-by in a quiet shopping street.

204

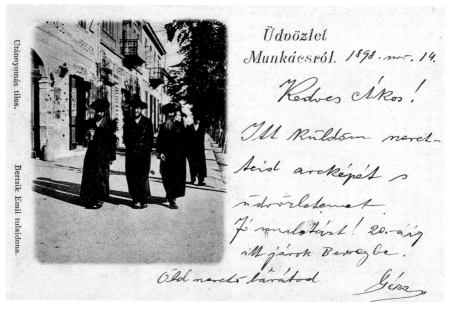

Hasidic Jews in the streets of Mukachevo.
Opposite: window shopping in Jvano Frankosk.

Stryj — Rynek — Ringplatz

Market day in Stryy.
Opposite: Jews apprehensively reading news from the front posted on the wall of the commander's office
in the square. Their apprehension was justified since the town was the theater of intense fighting between
the Russians and Germans. The resulting destruction, pillaging and repression affected the Jewish community particularly.

Juden lesen die neuesten Kriegsberichte vor der
Kommandantur in Stanislau.

Aus Galizien :   Am Stadtbrunnen

At a municipal well in Ternopol.
Opposite: the market square in Kosova.

210

The "Jewish street" in Kovel.

Wladimir-Wolynsk. Warschauer Laden.
Włodzimierz-Wołyński. Sklepy warszawskie.

Waiting for customers in a street of "Warsaw" shops, so-called
because their owners had come from Warsaw to seek their fortune in Vladimir-Volynskiy.

212

Jewish children in Kovel.

Jewish adolescents in the Carpathian Mountains, dressed very differently to their Belorussian or Polish counterparts.

M. Szigeti orth. zsidó

M. Sziget 1900
Je vous envoie cette
Carte Mademoiselle
pour vous faire voir
les gens avec qui
Je marchande
aussi Je vous assure
que cela me donne
toujours l'envie
de rester dans ce Joli

Mayer és Berger M. Sziget

217

Orthodox Jews in Sighet. Twenty-eight years after this card with its tendentious remarks
was posted, Elie Weisel was born in this town, renowned for its Hasidic community.
Opposite: a Jewish peasant having a bite to eat.

218

Poultry specialists negotiating.

A friendly discussion between a Romanian Jew and an Austrian army officer.

220

Verlag v. Leon König, Papierhdlg., Czernowitz.

No. 435.

Typen - Bilder aus Ostgalizien und der Bukowina.

Jewish peasants in a farmyard in Bukovina.
Opposite: a father with his sons in Sighet.
Following pages: young *yeshiva* students.

Máramarosi
zsidó
típusok

RESTAURANTS
SHOPS
TRADES

The Paul Mandel restaurant in Poznan.
Jews were often restaurateurs, particularly in
rural areas. At the turn of the century, some
made enough money to open brasseries
or restaurants in the towns.
Following pages: the shop of a prosperous
furrier, Cahn, in Riga, capital of Latvia.

МѢХОВОЙ
МАГАЗИНЪ.

PELZ
MAGAZIN.

S. CAHN.

Herrenstrasse

Verlag Schatz & Weinberg, Riga.

Riga.

Гродно.—Grodno. № 14.
Гостинный рядъ.

228

Grodno had one of Belorussia's oldest Jewish communities. In 1902, Jews comprised two-thirds of the population. The writing on the postcard reveals the anti-Semitism rife in the Russian empire at that time.
Opposite: a Jewish shop in Pribenik in Slovakia.

Üdvözlet Perbenyikről

230

A shop in Baranovici, then majority Jewish.
Opposite: Jewish shops in the Ukrainian villages of Povorsk and Kvasy.

Powursk.   Jüdisches Verkaufshaus mit Teestube.

Landschaft bei Unterberg

Paul Mandel's Waldrestaurant

An open-air restaurant near the village of Podvolochisk in the Ukraine.
Opposite: the forest annexe of Paul Mandel's restaurant.

234

In the ghetto in Bialystok. Most of the signs are in both Hebrew and German characters.

Albert Baum's grocer's shop in the town of Szczecin in Poland.

236

Warenkaufhaus Aronheim & Cohn, Stettin Gruss aus Stettin

237

The Aronheim & Cohn department store in Szczecin.
Opposite: the Barasch brothers' department store in Katowice.

238

Luxury shops in the Mikolascha arcade in the Ukrainian town of Lvov.
The Jews reigned over small businesses, from stall to prestigious shop.

Привѣтъ изъ Полтавы.
Писчебумажный магазинъ
И. А. Дохмана.

The Dochman stationery shop in Poltava, a small Ukrainian town with a particularly active Jewish community.

Pozdrowienie z Podwołoczysk.

Ulica kolejowa.

J. BLUMENFELD

240

Харьковъ. Сумская улица.

Throughout the Ukraine, the Jews demonstrated their commercial dynamism.
(Left, Podvolochisk and Kharkov; right, Kolomyya and Stryy.)

Kołomyja — Kolomea — Коломия
Rynek. — Ringplatz. — Ринок.

241

Stryj   Rynek

The Silber family in front of their shop in Kukzurmare, a small town in the Chernotsy region.

A door-to-door peddler selling *tallithim* (the prayer shawl worn by all devout Jews).
Following pages: the humble trades of the "Jewish street" disappeared forever with the annihilation of Yiddishland. These often colorful characters were a popular theme of the flourishing contemporary literature.

טַלִיתִים-הֶענדלער.

H.Goldberg

אידישע פרנסות״.

דער הענדלער (1).

אויסגעטהון פון זיך די שאנד, –

מיט א זעקעל אין דער האנד

געהט ער אום פון הויף צו הויף

הויבט די אויגען אלץ ארויף,

און װי טרויעריג ער זינגט

איבערן גאנצען הויף עס קלינג

האנדעל–האנדעל

א. רייזען.

ח. ג. אלד.

אידישע פרנסות.

‫— נו, לאָמיר אָקאָרשט נאָר בעטראַכטען די שמאַטע‬
‫הם... קודם — צוויי לעבער פאָרהאַן לעת־עתה, —‬
‫איצט, זעהט, די פאָדקלאַדקע — ס'א קריעה־וּבליה !‬
‫בכלל, וויפיעל קאָסט עס בּיי אייך די מציאה ?‬

Sausage "merchants".

KAIFEN SE SCHENE SACHENS

KRIWUS J.FELDE DEZ. 1916

Peddler: "Buy my fine wares".
Following pages: porters.

54950 Jüdischer Wasserträger

254

BARANOWITSCHI.   Russischer Wasserträger.

BARANOWITSCHI.   Russische jüdische Volkstypen.

Above, opposite and following pages: water carriers.
Preceding pages: peddlers of all manner of goods and a water carrier.

Krieg im Osten

Jüdische Wasserträger.

010 a

258

The well, obligatory meeting place and distillery of local gossip.

Винница. № 21.
Водовозъ Айзикъ и его сынъ Липа.

Jüd: Wasserverkäufer
im Grojec

Transporting barrels (probably containing kosher wine) by river and road.
Opposite: a water seller in the streets of Pinsk.

260

STRASSENBILD IN PINSK

261

262

Les ouvriers.

Société „Libanon" Varsovie. (47)   .חברה „לבנני" וואָרשא   פּוֹיעלים.

The Jewish carpenters' guild. Synagogues were built out of wood.

Horse dealers.

265

Originalaufnahme vom Kriegsschauplatz.
Der immer gern gesehene Marketender.

PHOTOCHEMIE.BERLIN
2862

Jewish traveling victuallers, here following the German army.

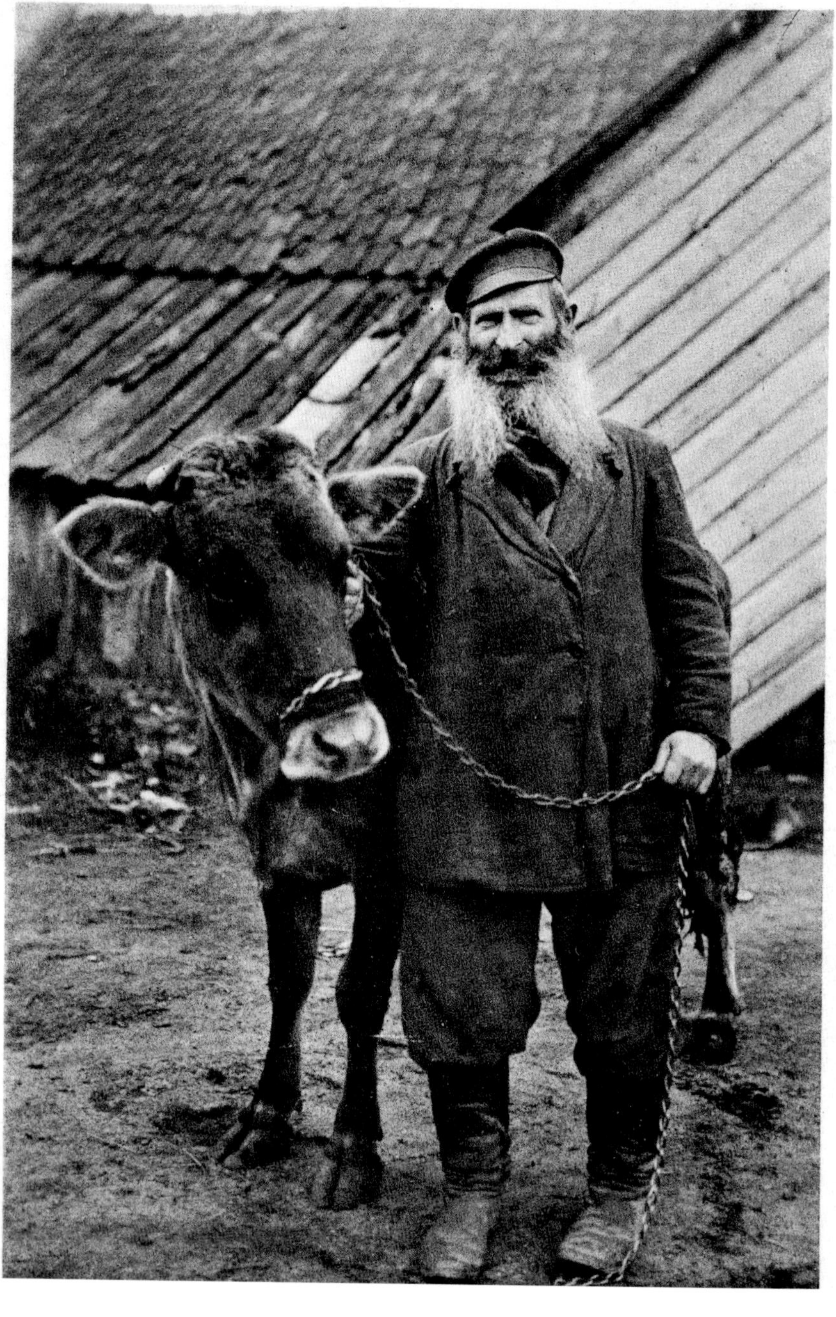

Cattle dealers.
Following pages: Jewish and native peddlers.
Children selling German newspapers in Louviez, fifty kilometers from Lodz.

Russische Händler-Typen in Mlawa.

Bird-catcher.
Preceding pages: newspaper sellers.

274

Candle sellers, market gardeners, second-hand dealers and butchers, all doing business with the German army.

Jüdische Händlerin
mit Wärmetopf

דער פֿישמאַרק.   מינקאָווסקי.

Fishwife.
Opposite: a woman selling hot soup.

278

Knife-grinders.

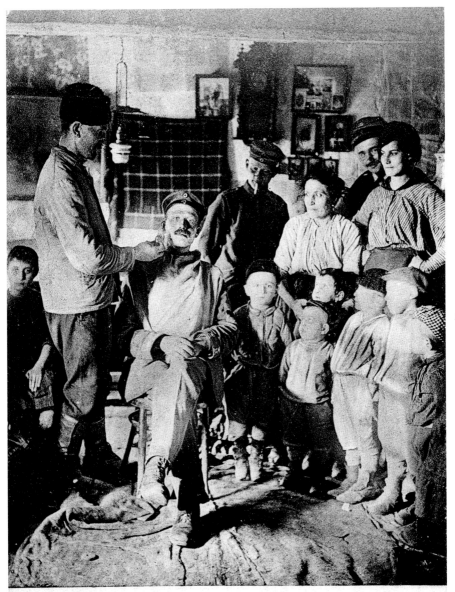

Der Krieg im Osten — Beim jüdischen Dorfbarbier

Barber.
Opposite: cobbler.

דער טאנדייטניק.

„אָט אַזױ נײהט אַ שנײַדער
אָט אַזױ נײהט ער צו ;
ער נײהט און נײהט אַ גאַנצע װאָך
און האָט אַ נאָדעל מיט אַ לאָד
אָט אַזױ נײהט אַ שנײַדער,
אָט אַזױ נײהט ער צו ."

פאָלקס־ליעדער.

H.GOLDBERG

Typy żydowskie
Jüdische Typen aus Russ. Polen

Second-hand shoe seller.
Opposite: tailor, with the well-known popular song "That's the way a tailor sews…"
Following double pages: fortune-tellers.
For decades, the humble trades of the "Jewish street" created the social and economic cohesion of Yiddishland.

סימָנים גענוג דא פאַרהאַן :
ווּעסט נעהמען אַ כַּלה אַ גאָלד, אַ בריליאַנט
דערצו אויך — אַ גרויסען נָדַן !

H. GOLDBERG.

לשנה טוב

לשנה טובה

וועסט געהמען אַ חתן גאָר איינס אין דער וועלט, —
פון הימעל דיר איז עס בעשערט:
וועסט האבען אי קליידער, אי ציערונג, אי געלד,
און אַלץ, וואָס דאָס האַרץ נאָר בעגעהרט !...

ח. גאָלדבערג

Dreikaiserreichsecke

Kaufleute auf Reisen in Russ. Polen

SCHOOLS
HOSPITALS
HOSPICES
CEMETERIES

Portraits of the teachers at the Hebraic school in
Ukmerge in Lithuania for the 1932 school year.
Following pages: pupils of the Tahut Hebraic
school in Ukmerge.

Schaulen.   Talmud Thora

г. Минскъ — 3-е Женское Еврейское училище

Munsk — 3-ime école juive pour jeunes filler

294

The Talmud Tora of Siauliai (Shavli) in Lithuania.
The Jewish young girls' school in Minsk in Belorussia. Jewish state schools were not mixed.

Могилевъ-Под. Казенное еврейское училище.
L'école israélite de l'état.

Бобруйскъ. Прогимназія Лазаревой.

The state school for boys in Mogilev.
The Jewish school in Bobruysk in Belorussia.

בית ספר
תושיה
ליברמן

Tsvi-Hirch Liberman's Tishiah school.
Following pages: a school integrated into the Tarbut, an educational and cultural organization particularly active in eastern Europe. This network of primary and secondary schools, whose pupils were taught in Hebrew, was banned by the authorities at the beginning of the Soviet regime.

The *yeshiva* in Lida in Belorussia, founded in 1905 by Isaac Jacob Reines, the first president of the Mizrahi religious Zionist movement. Founded in Vilnius in 1902, the organization took root in several European countries. After the Russian Revolution of 1905, repression and pogroms forced the movement to transfer its head office first to Frankfurt then to Eretz Israel.

The famous *yeshiva* in Lublin, founded in 1930 by Rabbi Meir Shapira.

Одесса.—Odessa. № 105.
Еврейская общественная больница.—L'hôpital public israélite.

Eastern European Jews had a network of hospitals reserved for their communities. In Odessa, as in all medical establishments elsewhere, patients ate kosher food, thereby respecting the dietary requirements of Jewish law.

A Jewish school in Miedzyrzec Podlaski (Mezrich in Yiddish).
Around ten thousand Jews lived in this Polish town ninety kilometers north of Lublin.

Dom kolonii izraelickiej w Rabce.

The summer camp in Rabka, for the children of Kraków.

Verwaltungsgebäude

Wirtschaftsgebäude

Israelitisches Krankenhaus Breslau

Hauptgebäude (Südfront)

Hauptgebäude (Westfront)

The imposing Jewish medical center in Wroclaw (formerly Breslau) in Poland.

308

Judenschule in Polen

From *heder* to *yeshiva*, some Jews studied ceaselessly. For centuries, rabbis have studied the sacred texts for an exegesis of the divine message, the most famous among them originating intellectual movements which still have disciples today.

77 St . . . In der Judenschule

310

Ковель   Еврейская Больница

Nahman Bialik Jewish hospital in Belaya Tserkov, seventy kilometers south of Kiev.
Jewish hospital in Kovel.

A classroom in 1930 in the Jewish orphanage in the Ukrainian town
of Gorodenka, which was particularly well endowed with community facilities.

Östliches Kriegsbild.
Jüdischer Friedhof in Wilkowischken.

312

The Jewish cemetery in Vilkaviskis in Lithuania.
The Jewish cemetery in Brasov in Romania.

482

ALTER JUDENFRIEDHOF BEI SLONIM   PHOT. E. BENNINGHOVEN

313

Grabsteine auf dem jüdischen Friedhofe in Brest-Litowsk.
Oktober 1915.

188

The Jewish cemetery in Sionim in Belorussia.
Steles in the Jewish cemetery in Brest Litovsk in Belorussia.

Polish Jews in the cemetery in Piotrkow Trybunalski. The steles decorated with a candlestick with three, five or seven branches signify sepulchres of women, whose task it is to light the candles on the Sabbath. Opposite: a stele in the Jewish cemetery in Suwalki in Poland, in memory of Sagdar, son of Avrom Alessandrowicz, who died on 9 Kislev 5665 (November 17th, 1904 in the Gregorian calendar).

A German soldier at a grave in the Jewish cemetery in Jaunjelgava in Latvia.
The lion above the stone's inscription signifies the grave of someone called Arie or Lejb.
The lion can also signify belonging to the Jewish people.

A visit to the cemetery in Nizhniye Vereski in the Ukraine.
Overgrown vegetation in Jewish cemeteries is not due to neglect
but tradition, which forbids the pulling up of brambles and weeds.

SYNAGOGUES

At dawn, the *chames* knocks on the shutters
of the sleeping faithful, crying, "To the synagogue,
to the synagogue!" The Jewish street then fills up with
orthodox observers of Mosaic law.
These pictures are all the more moving because, by razing
the synagogues, Hitler's followers were intentionally
destroying a place of worship, a symbol of Jewish presence
and a depository of memories. The Nazis believed
the more or less systematic demolishing of synagogues
to be an ideological necessity and "The Crystal Night"
of November 9th, 1938, became the dress rehearsal
of wholesale destruction.

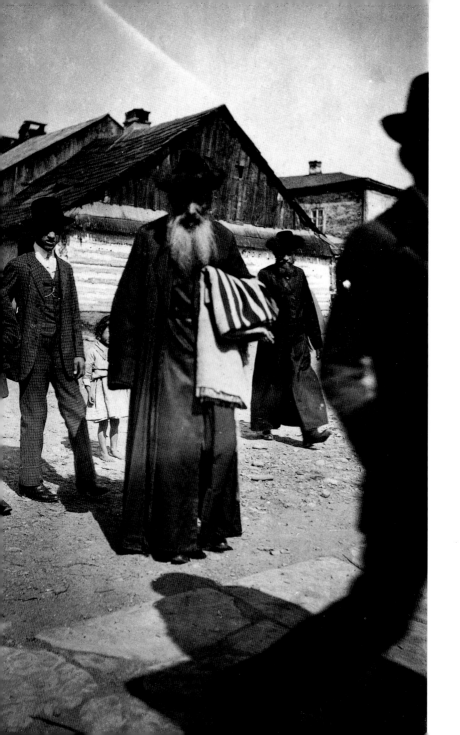

Verlag F. Blechmann, Mitau

The Synagogue of Jelgava, former capital of Courland.
Opposite: returning from morning prayer at the synagogue,
a worshipper stops to pose for a war correspondent in the Kaiser's army.
Following pages: the synagogue in Jurbarkas. Built in the 18th century, it escaped the frenetic
destruction by the German army and their Lithuanian collaborators during the Second World War.
Preceding pages: typical daily scenes in the *shtetl* under the German occupation during the First World War.

JURBURG

SYNAGOGA

IROKI. Karaimska Kenesa

Frauenburg. Sunagoge

A Karaite synagogue in the Trakai area near Vilnius. A Judaic sect opposed by rabbis since its creation, the Karaites rejected Talmudic and Rabbinic tradition, advocating a doctrine of strict adherence to Judaism's biblical sources. **T**he synagogue in Saldus, Latvia.

Synagoge in Prenÿ

327

Wilkowischky, Synagoge

Gegründet im Jahre 5305
Remontiert im Jahre 5670

לשנה טובה תכתבו ותחתמו

The synagogue in Prienai.
The synagogue in Vilkaviskis, dating from the 16th century.

328

The synagogue in Bolshiye Luki.
The synagogue in Minsk.

329

The synagogue in Minsk was almost
completely destroyed during the First World War.

330

г. Мстиславль Могилевской губ. № 8.
Синагога.

Synagogue of the *shtetl* of Mstislavi, whose population at the turn of the century was more than half Jewish.

331

The synagogue in Bereza.

332

The synagogue in Ozery, dating from the 17th century.

333

Uralte hölzerne Synagoge in Jeziory bei Grodno

The synagogue in Grodno, built in the 18th century. During the First World War, the town's population was two-thirds Jewish.

334

Лунно, Грод. губ.   Старинная еврейская синагога

The synagogue in Lunna.

Jüdischer Tempel in Jwje

335

The synagogue in the small town of Ivye, which was three-quarters Jewish under the German occupation during the First World War.

336

The fortified synagogue in Lyuboml, built in the 16th century.

PIŃSK. Wielka Synagoga.

The main synagogue in Pinsk, built in 1640. Between 1900 and 1920, three-quarters of the city's population were Jews.

338

135. Гомель, Большая синагог

The synagogue in Gomel, built in the mid-19th century.
Opposite: inaugurated in 1887, the grand synagogue of Gdansk, then Danzig, was burned down by the Nazis during the "Kristallnacht", on November 9th, 1938, and definitively razed to the ground in 1939.

340

Hindenburg O.-S. — Synagoge

The synagogue in Zabrze, built in 1865.

Bendzin - Będzin   Burg u. Synagoge · Zamek i Synagoga

341

The synagogue in Bedzin, burned down by the Nazis when they entered the town on September 4th, 1939. They also set fire to neighboring houses belonging to Jews.

342

Żółkiew   Synagoga

The synagogue in Zolkiew, whose construction in the town center was refused by
the authorities, who even went as far as dictating the style of this fortified building.
Opposite: built in the second half of the 19th century, the imposing synagogue in Poznan was used as
a stable by the German army in 1939. The building's desecration was consecrated in an official ceremony
during which the occupying authorities symbolically removed the Star of David from the central dome.

Posen   Die neue Synagoge

343

344

The synagogue in Jaslo, whose Jewish community represented more than 20% of the population during the First World War.

DĄBROWA. - Synagoga.

345

The synagogue in Dabrowa Gomicza.

One of the numerous synagogues in Warsaw.

Warszawa. Synagoga.

The grand synagogue in Tlomacka Street in Warsaw. Designed by an Italian architect, it was finished in 1878 and blown up by the Nazis in 1943.

348

A chapel built by Russian Jews in a hut in the prison camp in Dabie during the First World War.
Opposite: the painted ceiling of a synagogue in Kazimierz Dolny.
Following pages: outside the synagogue in Latczyn.

STARÓŻYTNA SYNAGOGA W KAZIMIERZU

352

The synagogue in Sniadowo.

Der 700jährige Holzbau der Synagoge in Przedborz

The synagogue in Przedborz, built around 1760.

Katowice — Świątynia Żydowska — *Synagogue*

Kazimierz Dolny. Góra Trzech Krzyży i Synagoga.

355

A synagogue on the outskirts of Kazimierz Dolny.
Opposite: the Grand Synagogue in Katowice, built at the end of the 19th
century. Around 3,000 Jews lived there on the eve of the First World War.

The synagogue in Ostrowiecz, in the province of Kielce.

The synagogue in Lanckrorona, a village thirty kilometers from Kraków.

CHODORÓW. Bóżnica z XVII. wieku.

The synagogue in Khodorov.

Будівництво цівільне.
Божниця караїмська в Луцьку.
Фотогр. М. Черкавського.

The synagogue in Lutsk, Volhynia.

The synagogue in Zdolbunov.

Judentempel in G.

The synagogue in Gorokhov.

Винница. № 18.
Главная Синагога.—Głuwna synagoga.

A synagogue in the Vinnitsa ghetto.

Wladimir-Wolynsk. Schulstraße mit Synagoge.
Włodzimierz-Wołyński. Synagoga na ulicy Szkolnej.

Polish peasant women selling their produce outside the synagogue in Vladimir-Wolynskiy,
where the Jewish community represented half the population during the First World War.

Synagogues in Vizhnitsa, a renowned Hasidic center.

Przed bóżnicą

Przed bóżnicą

One of the many synagogues in Lvov, a town with well-structured orthodox and Zionist communities.

366

31. Чуфутъ Кале. Близъ Бахчисарая.
Караимская (синагога.
Tchufut-Kale, près de Baktsisarai.
La Synagogue Caraime.

A Karaite synagogue in Chufut Kale.

Луцкъ — Еврейская Синагога
Łuck — Synagoga żydowska

367

The synagogue in Lutsk, fortified in order to defend the town's
inhabitants against attacks by Tartars and Cossacks.

Synagoga-Synagoge   BRODY·

368

Built in the 17th century, the fortified synagogue in Brody withstood the ravages
of time and men for nearly three hundred years until the SS razed it in 1943.

Хоральная Синагога.   Кишиневъ.

369

The synagogue in Kishinev, capital of Moldavia,
rendered sadly famous by the pogroms of 1903 and 1905.

RELIGION

FESTIVITIES

לשנה טובה תכתבו

MEILLEURS VŒUX POUR LA NOUVELLE ANNÉE

Greeting cards for Rosh Hashana (the Jewish New Year)
were written in Yiddish or Hebrew. The captions
were often humorous. The themes were drawn from
daily life and religion, their characteristic common
denominator on numerous cards being the phrase,
Shana Tova Tikatevou (a good year, so that it
shall be written, by God, in the Book of Life).
Following pages: greetings for the New Year
(Rosh Hashana), that is to say Happiness and Health.
Best New Year's wishes for body and soul.

עם טראָגט, עס ברעֶנגט דער נײ-יאָר טרעֶגער
פֿונמעֶן, משעקן און כּל-טוב,
בּשורות טובֿות און נחמות,
פֿאַר דעֶם גײסט און פֿאַר דעֶם גוף.

Most greeting cards produced by the publishing house Yehudia were drawn by a *yeshiva* pupil, Hayyim Goldberg, who also wrote the Yiddish texts. He was murdered by the Nazis in 1943.

לשנה טובה תכתבו.

וואכט אווף, א נייער יאהר איצט געהט!
נאט שליסט אווף אוצרות מאכט און פרייד,
און ימים גליק וועט ער צונעבען,
און ליכטיג מאכט ער אייך דאס לעבען !

New Year's greetings. "Sincere best wishes: happiness and joy and may every day be one of light to brighten your existence."
Opposite: New Year's greetings. An ark full of the fruits of happiness, joy and good luck.

New Year's greetings. "May the year to come bring you joy, happiness, light…"
Opposite: "What is the New Year bringing the little children? Look what's falling!
Happiness and joy and ever more beautiful flowers…"

דורך ראדיאָ אַ ברכה
דער מאמען און דער שוועסטער.
זאָל זיין פֿאַר אַנזער דער יאָר
דער רייכסטער און דער בעסטער

לשנה טובה תכתבו

לשנה טובה תכתבו

פֿאָסט רעסטאַנט

פֿון. אים צו איר אַ בריוועלע,
אַ מאָונג מיט ליבע ווערטער :
.סטראַג בליק, דו נייער יאָר, אַ סך
פֿאַר איר — פֿאַר מיין באַשערטער !"

"That this year be the most fruitful, the best."
"Dingaling! - Hello, who's there? - Me, your sweetheart. Darling, I wish every joy and happiness for the new year."
Opposite: greetings from a young man to his intended, with all his love...

Kapparot. A chicken is rotated three times over the head of each participant
while an expiatory prayer is recited. It is believed that this ritual, practiced
by certain orthodox Jews on the eve of Yom Kippur, transfers the sins of
the participants to the fowl, which is then sacrificed and given to the poor.
Following pages: Yom Kippur. The most observed festivity, even by non-practicing
Jews, during which a twenty-four-hour fast and continual presence at
the synagogue allow the believer hope of God's forgiveness for the sins
committed during the previous year.
During the service, the penitents of Yom Kippur beat their heart as a sign
of repentance at the mention of each sin by the officiating rabbi.

לשנה טובה

דער האָהן ער געהמ צום טוימ אַצונד,
און מיר—צום לעבען און געזונד...

384

Gang zum Tempel   (Jom Kiper)

Verlag v. Schiller. Czernowitz No. 101

פערנעהם מיין הייסע תפלה,
דו מלך חַיֵנקִים,
און שיק אונז, שיק דיין ברכה,
צום יָאהר, צום יָאהר צום נייעם!

לשנה טובה.

Segen am Versöhnungstage *1903 Jassy*

Kippur. The head of the family blesses his next of kin.

The *shohet*, a sacrificer who specialized in the ritual slaughter of animals according to the rituals of the *kashrut*.

388

Galiz. Jude
beim Gebet.

7. Seppl-Gasse in Iwanowo
während des Laubhüttenfestes 1916.

Sukkot in Ivanova in the Ukraine in 1916. The sky could
be seen through the roof flaps as in a traditional *sukka*.
The faithful lived for seven days in a furnished space beneath the roof.
Opposite: Shaharit, or morning prayer, which every practicing Jew
must recite with the phylacteries attached to the left arm and forehead.
Following pages: construction of a *sukka* before the celebration of Sukkot on the fifteenth
day of the month of Tishri. This festivity commemorates the halt of the Hebrews in the desert after
their march out of Egypt. The hut must be inhabited for seven days.
The palm branch, or *lulav*, and citron, or *etrog*, used during the festival of Sukkot.

בַּסֻּכֹּת תֵּשְׁבוּ שִׁבְעַת יָמִים.

לשנה טובה.

Der Krieg im Osten
Klagende Judenweiber

Beerdigung eines angesehenen Juden in Lida

392

Professional mourners going to the cemetery.
The burial of a respected Jew in Lida. The body is being carried on a stretcher
through the *shtetl*, from his home to the cemetery, by four men.

Am Schabbes in Bialystock

393

Concert given by a German army band on the Sabbath for Jews in Bialystok.
Shabbat, day of rest.
Following pages: fishing on Friday morning for the meal on Shabbat.

Lighting the candles on Shabbat, the task of women.

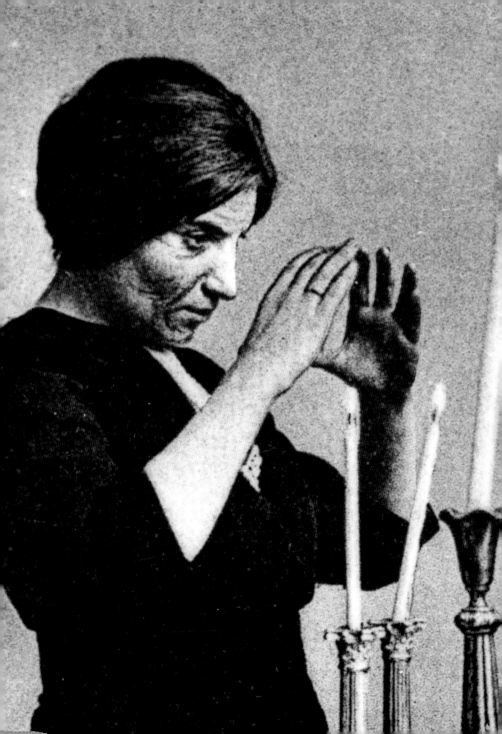

398

Wherever he may be and under any circumstances, the practicing Jew
begins each day by reciting a prayer, having attached his phylacteries,
the black leather boxes containing Torah texts, to his left arm and forehead.

Following pages: a Talmudist student, well-versed in the scriptures.
She reads the Bible in Yiddish for women.

Talmud chochem.

פסח צום סדר ביי דייטשע אידען.

הסדר.

During the *seder*, the meal of Pesah (Passover), everyone relives, through the texts, the Hebrews' flight from Egypt. Certain items on the menu are based on symbolic prescriptions.

405

Aspiring Talmudists.

S. M. P. Kraków Deposé 1902

Schadchen i Machetunim

S. M. P. Kr. Deposé 1902

Maseltow Tate! Man Kale ist Tabele!

The *shadkhan*, or go-between, introducing the fiancés, and the happy conclusion of the "transaction".
Opposite: two different paths, one faith.

Gruss aus der Bukowina.

Palais des Wunderrabbi in Sadagóra. 27/8

grand merci pour la carte.
Avec beaucoup de compliments
Dr Anne Hulles n.291.

409

Ottynia — Оттинія
Rabbiners Wohnhaus — Mieszkanie rab.

Certain rabbis, generally Hasidic, were such prestigious teachers that full-fledged courts
grew up around them. Disciples and the faithful came from far afield to receive
the benediction of these holy men, who possessed beautiful homes, or veritable palaces.

Tashlik, the ceremony on the banks of a river or stream celebrating the first day of Rosh Hashana (corresponding to the Christian New Year). The faithful recite a prayer whilst turning their pockets inside out, thereby signifying that they are getting rid of their sins by passing them on to the fish.

Gebet bei Vollmond.

סִימָן טוֹב יִטַּזָּל טוֹב יְהֵא לָנוּ וּלְכָל יִשְׂרָאֵל אָמֵן:

The prayer to the moon is recited on the third night after the full moon, providing it is clearly visible. This ritual symbolizes the renewal of nature, the work of God.

Feldrabbiner Dr. Frankfurter beim Gottesdienst der russischen Kriegsgefangenen in Bruck-Kiralyhida. 1915

413

A religious service being carried out by a German army chaplain,
Dr Frankfurter, in a prison camp for Russian soldiers behind the Austro-Hungarian lines.

414

Military chaplains of the three religions.

Jewish soldiers in the Kaiser's army posing with their rabbi in a village on the eastern front.

416

A religious service in the countryside, conducted by an army chaplain,
Dr Sonderling, from Hamburg, in September 1914.

Originalaufnahme vom Kriegsschauplatz 1915

Jüdischer Feldgeistlicher
(Dr. Sonderling aus Hamburg)

A convoy of Jewish refugees fleeing Russian counter-attacks
to reach the protection provided by the German army.

Eine Überfuhr über den „Sanfluss" zur österr.-russischen Grenze.

419

Refugees crossing from Russia to Austria on an Austrian army pontoon.

Die zerstörte Stadt Josefow an der Weichsel. Im Hintergrund eine von Oesterreichern geschlagene Notbrücke.

420

The *shtetl* of Dejozefow, on the banks of the Vistula, destroyed during the fighting.

After the fighting, Polish-Russian Jewish refugees returned to ruins and famine.

CULTURE

POLITICS

Galician chess players painted by Kaufmann.
The Jews, following the example of King Solomon,
have always been passionate adepts of this game
and have produced many of its masters.

424

Ch. Slonimsky.

.ח. ז. סלונימסקי (חז"ס)

Hayyim Selig Sionimski, born in 1834 in Bialystok, author of works on astronomy and a painstaking analyst of the Hebrew calendar, in which he discovered a number of errors.

AUS DEM BUCHE JÜDISCHE KÜNSTLER

LESSER URY

Lesser Ury, painter, born in Miedzychod (then Bimbaum) in 1861, creator of the famous work, *Jerusalem*, depicting the plight of homeless Jews fleeing the Tsarist regime.

426

Antoine **RUBINSTEIN**, compositeur
né à Vechvotynetz en 1829
Oeuvres : Lalla Rookh, Dimitri Douskoi, Chasseur
de Sibérie, des Oratorios, des Symphonies, des
Ouvertures, des Sonates, etc.

Anton Grigoryevich Rubinstein, born in 1829 in the Ukraine. Some of his
operas were inspired by his Jewish origins despite his parents' conversion.

WLADIMIR HOROWITZ
Pianiste

Vladimir Horowitz, pianist of genius, born in Kiev in 1904.

Ch. N. Bialik

ח. נ. ביאליק.

חברת "לבנון" No 74

Eliezer Yitzhak Perelmann, alias Ben Yehouda, born in Luzhky
in 1858, lexicographer of genius who "invented" modern Hebrew.
Opposite: Hayyim Nahmann Bialik, born in 1873 in Radi
in the Ukraine. The greatest Jewish poet of our time to have written in both
Yiddish and Hebrew, his influence on modern authors is considerable.

The triumphal performance of *The Dybbuk* in the 1920s by the Habimah troupe.
The play by Solomon Zainwill Rappaport, better known as S. Ansky, was first
performed by this Yiddish troupe from Vilnius in 1920. It has since been translated
into numerous languages, including Hebrew, French, English and German.
Opposite and following pages: actors of the Yiddish theater.

М-ме Гольдштейнъ.
M-me GOLDSZTEJN.

WID. M.L.RICHNERA
w ŁODZI

8.

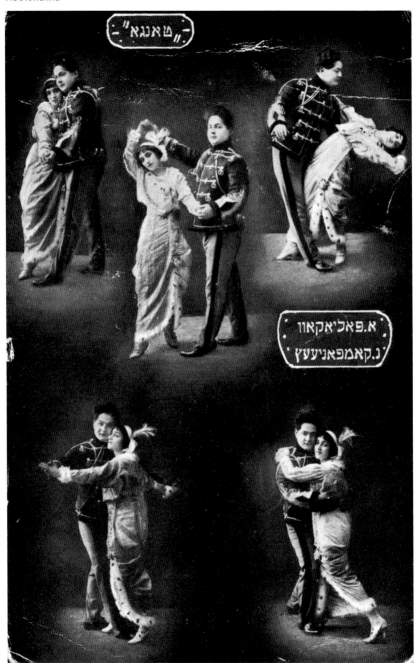

Напуги въ Сіонъ. Ребъ-Хононъ - К. В. Бравичъ
Dr. театръ.
Не то еврей, не то не еврей. хочетъ въ Сіонъ, и въ Мессію не
вѣритъ; говоритъ на святомъ языкѣ, и ходитъ безъ шапки.

434

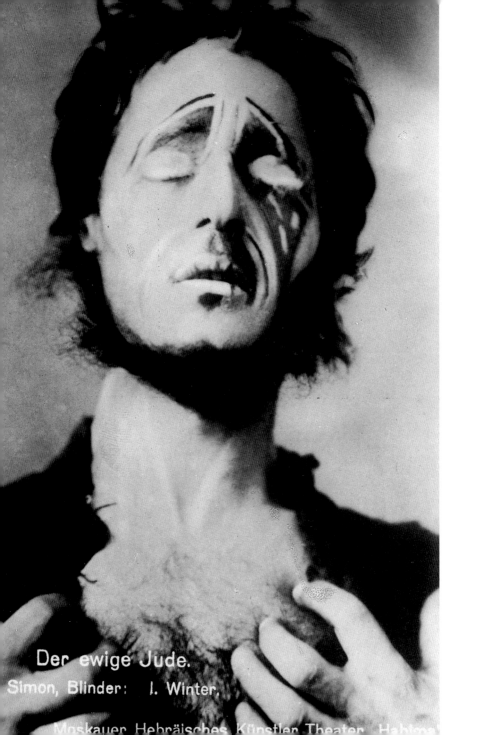

Der ewige Jude.

Simon, Blinder: I. Winter.

Moskauer Hebräisches Künstler-Theater "Habima"

Esther Rachel Kaminska, a star of the Polish Yiddish theater, nicknamed the Yiddish Sarah Bernhardt.
Opposite: a timeless Jew in the Yiddish theater in Moscow.

Ai wai! Der gestorbene Kümft!

A humorous scene from the Yiddish theater: "Ah, ah, ah, death returns!"
Opposite: Boris Thomashefsky, born in 1868 in the Ukraine, pioneer of Yiddish theater in the United States.

439

Борисъ Томашевскiй
B. Tomaszewski

Wyd. M.L. Richnera
w Łodzi

440

314

ARTIST OF THE HABAMAH HAIVRITH.

משחק מהבמה העברית.

יודישע ביהנע

דראנאװ

441

Dranov, actor of the Yiddish theater.
Opposite: an actor of the famous Yiddish theater troupe, Habimah,
founded in Moscow in 1917 and which moved to Palestine in 1931.

Ghettopolitiker.

L. Krestin.

Reading news of the world in the *shtetl*.
Opposite: the violinist, one of Yiddishland's emblematic characters.

Polish, Yiddish and Hebraic newspapers, selected by the Warsaw publisher, Lebanon: *Die Welt, Folkstaytung, Freie Welt, Yiddish Volksblatt, Ha Kol, Ha Yom* and *Ha Karmel.*

Мозырь, Минск. губ. Mosir.

Рабочій Каганъ, звѣрски убитъ въ тюрьмѣ въ день
объявленія конституціи. Выстрѣломъ у него снятъ былъ
черепъ, а потомъ былъ добитъ прикладомъ

"In memory of our fallen soldiers. At Minsk, on Constitution Day in 1906, the worker Kagan was brutally murdered in prison. After his skull was smashed his body was exhibited as an example."

A banner carried by members of the Bund during a march to commemorate the Revolution: "The Democratic Republic forever...Long live international socialism."

448

אומגאב פֿון בונד, 1905.

A card published by the Bund, "Abe Reich died aged seventeen, killed during a demonstration in Dvinsk on March 4th, 1905. Shlomo Margolin, aged twenty-two, mortally wounded during a demonstration in Warsaw on April 2nd, 1905, died on April 5th. E.Cohen, murdered during the same demonstration."

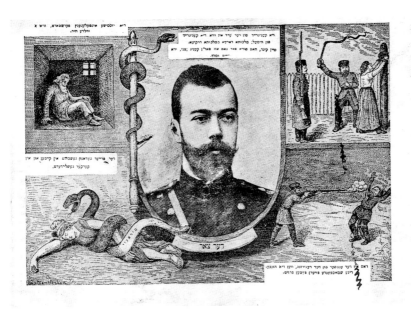

Portrait of Tsar Nicholas II, held responsible for the horrors of the 1905 pogroms.
The hanging of a revolutionary in Warsaw in 1905. "The result of an autocratic and bureaucratic regime which violently repressed student protests, broke demonstrators' ribs, and organized the pogroms against Jews and Armenians."

Karl I. im befreiten Kolomea

450

1916: a delegation from the Jewish community in Kolomyya welcoming Charles I,
Emperor of Austria and King of Hungary, to the Ukrainian town, liberated by his troops.
Opposite: Rosa Luxemburg, born in 1871 in Zamosc in Poland. She took part in the 1905
revolution in Warsaw, and at the end of 1918 created the Spartacus League, which became the German
Communist Party. She was assassinated on January 15th, 1919 by officers escorting her to a Berlin prison.

452

Children from a Jewish school in Minsk on May 1st, 1931,
marching with the banner, "Working class children from all countries".

Members of the Histadrut of Horondenka, a radical
Jewish trade union movement, at its founding in 1920.
Members of a left-wing Zionist movement in Lubelski.

454

Workers, members of the Histadrut.
Following pages: an outing in the Ostrog forest in the Ukraine.
A party organized by the Bund in Dvinsk, Lithuania, in 1930. A group of Zionists posing under the banner, "Long live the socialist movement in Palestine!"

Girl members of the Zionist group, Freiheit, in Poland in 1927.
Opposite: Chaïm Weizmann, born in 1874 in the Belorussian
shtetl of Motol. A biochemist by training, he led the international
Zionist organization and was the first president of Israel.
Following pages: somewhere in Poland, members of Betar,
a Zionist activist youth movement, begun in Riga in 1923.

302

CHAIM WEIZMAN

חיים ויצמן

464

The flag and uniformed members of Betar in Mariampol in Lithuania. This Zionist youth movement, accused by its political opponents of being fascist, based its ideology on the rebirth of a majority Jewish state on both banks of the River Jordan.
Opposite: Vladimir Jabotinsky, born in 1880 in Odessa. Having, in 1917, formed a Jewish legion to fight alongside the British to liberate Palestine from the Ottoman yoke, in 1925 he founded the World Union of Revisionist Zionists, then subsequently, in 1935, the New Zionist Organization. An intransigent hard-liner, he occasionally "dined with the devil" to achieve his goal, the establishment of a "Great Israel", in which all citizens would speak Hebrew.

WLADIMIR JABOTINSKY ואב ז'בוטינסקי

Members of the Ciechocinek branch of Centos in 1933. This federation of Polish Orphanage Aid Associations was born out of the progressive withdrawal of the American Jewish Joint Distribution Committee around 1924. Centos administrated orphanages, schools, summer camps and children's homes up until the Second World War.

ANTI-SEMITISM
POGROMS
ANTI-JEWISH
ORGANIZATIONS

Tsar Nicholas II, held responsible for
the pogroms which turned Russia into
a bloodbath, became the focus
of attacks by human rights activists
eager for his deposition.

Wekslarze krakowscy. — Krakauer Geldwechsler.

Money-changers in Kraków. Caricaturists perpetuated the anti-Semitic tradition of portraying Jews with ugly features and as money merchants.

471

473

Were these French people anti-Semitic before they visited the Ukraine, or did they become so while they were there?
Opposite: Jews were accused of spinning a huge spider's web all over the world through the press. On the back of the card:

Grasping, repugnant, avaricious,
This noxious and horrible reptile,
Wants, as is his custom,
To govern the fine land of Poland...
So, Poles, open your eyes!

474

La ville de Léopol est moitié
peuplée par ces sales Juifs.
Germaine

Polish anti-Semitic portraits, precursors of the Nazi propaganda cards.

Towards the end of 1904, the Union of the Russian People, a virulently anti-Semitic organization openly supported by the Tsar and his government, was founded in Russia. Its militia, the Black Hundreds, led by Purishkevich and Dubrovin, were largely responsible for the 1905 pogroms.

z Krwawych dni.

I współbraci naszych, Żydów
Dotknął klęski ogrom:
Dzicz kozacka, łupu chciwa
Sprawia krwawy pogrom.

478   La Russie pittoresque (Kishineff)

CARTE POSTALE

Ce côté est exclusivement réservé à l'adresse

13.5

M.r Braun

Deputé

Palais Bourbon

In Kishinev on April 6th and 7th, 1903, around fifty Jews were massacred and five hundred more wounded. The pogrom was preceded by a hate campaign built around an accusation of ritual murder. French observers sent photographs back to members of the French parliament with the ironic caption, "picturesque Russia".

La Russie pittoresque (Kichinett)

479

CARTE POSTALE

Ce côté est exclusivement réservé à l'adresse

13.5

10

Mr Morlot   Député

90, Boulevard Magenta

480

Several of the 300 Jews massacred in Odessa during the 1905 pogrom.

Anti-Semitic unrest in Warsaw: "In the sweet land of Russia," comments the correspondent.

482

ЖЕРТВЫ ЕВРЕЙСКАГО ПОГРОМА.

Some victims were covered with their prayer shawls.

Die von den Russen zerstörten Thora-Rollen in Sochaczew

Torah scrolls soiled by the Russians during the fighting in the town of Sochaczew in 1915.

Grausam hingeschlachtete jüdische Kinder in Jekaterinoslaw

הערויסגעגעבען פֿאן דער זעלבסטוועהר דער סאצ.דעמ. ארבייטער־פֿארטיי פֿועלי־ציון

Herausgegeben von der Selbstwehr-Org. d. soz.-dem. Arbeiter-Partei „Poale Zion"

Corpses of children slain during the pogrom in October 1915 in Yekaterinoslav. Armed self-defense units, formed after the 1903 massacres by the left-wing movement Paole Zion, tried to protect the community.

Wir leben nicht mehr in einer Zeit, wo wir die Juden in's Wasser werfen durften.
(Premier-Minister Carp in der rumän. Deputiertenkammer.)

Judenelend.

Im Jahre 1866 wurden diese Juden von den rumänischen Behörden „als Vagabunden" in Jassy aufgegriffen, nach Galatz gebracht und über die Donau auf türkisches Gebiet geschafft. Als die Türken ihnen nicht ohne Weiteres Aufnahme gewähren wollten, wurden diese Juden von den rumänischen Soldaten auf Befehl ihrer Vorgesetzten in die Donau geworfen. Einer ertrank, die anderen wurden von den Türken gerettet. Einer der Ueberlebenden wurde wahnsinnig.

Jews arrested in Jassy (Iasi) by the Romanians and thrown into the rivers by soldiers under orders from their officers. One of these Jews was drowned, another went mad after being saved by the Turks.

בילדער פֿון דעם פֿאַנראָמירטען באַברויסקער געגענט : אַ סאַניטאַרע אָבטיילונג פֿון דער געזעלשאַפֿט
צו פֿאַרהיטען דאָם געזונט פֿון דער אידישער באַפֿעלקערונג („אָזע").

Photographies prises dans la région pogromée de Bobrouisk : Un détachement sanitaire de la *Société de Protection de la Santé des Juifs* (OZE)

Photographs taken in the pogromed district of Bobrouisk : A sanitary detachment of the *Society for the protection of Jewish health* (OZE)

Doctors and nurses sent to the pogrom areas by the Aid Committee.

1. Израильсонъ, 2. Шрифтеликъ, 3. Соколинскій, 4. Анна Розенталь, 5. Гельманъ, 6. Никифоровъ, 7. Кастелянцъ, 8. Погосовъ, 9. Джехадзе, 10. Павелъ Розенталь, 11. Кудринъ, 12. Бодневскій, 13. Трифоновъ, 14. М. Лурье, 15. Хацкелевичъ, 16. Н. Каганъ, 17. Добромысловъ, 18. Доброжгенадзе, 19. Ржонца, 20. Фридъ, 21. Мѣдяникъ, 22. Камермахеръ, 23. Оржеровскій, 24. Ройтенштернъ, 25. Ольштейнъ, 26. Рудавскій, 27. Курнатовскій, 28. Цукеръ, 29. Ис. Ройзманъ, 30. Лейкинъ, 31. Мисюкевичъ, 32. Айзенбергъ, 33. Ченчехадзе, 34. Гинзбургъ, 35. Броудо, 36. Тепловъ, 37. Законъ, 38. Перазичъ, 39. Теслеръ, 40. Зараховичъ, 41. Рубинчикъ, 42. Ек. Ройзманъ, 43. Гоброкидзе, 44. Журавель, 45. Рабиновичъ, 46. О. Викеръ, 47. Д. Викеръ, 48. Лаговскій, 49. Гельфандъ, 50. Виноградовъ, 51. Вардоянцъ, 52. Г. Лурье, 53. Костюшко, 54. Жмуркина, 55. Дроновъ, 56. Залкиндъ.

Изданіе Бунда. 1904.

489

A self-defense group in Iakoutsk.

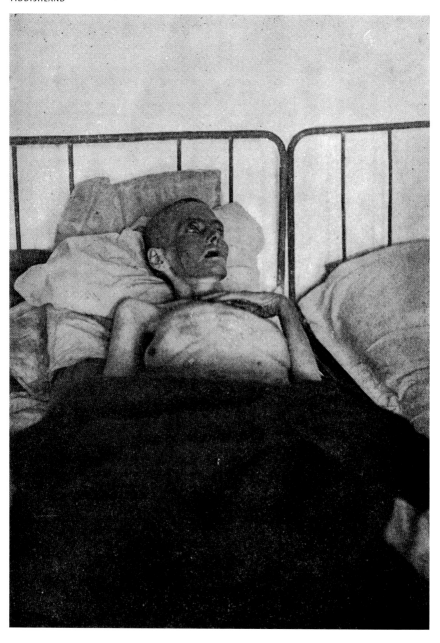

490

Corpses of famine victims being unloaded outside the gates
of the cemetery in the town of Nikolayev in the Ukraine.
Opposite: a young cachectic woman in hospital in Nikolayev,
a province whose Jewish population was ravaged by famine in 1922.

A meeting of Latvians of German origin during the Second World War.
These Nazis took part in the hunting down and mass murder of the Jews.

The SS training policemen on the eastern front in 1941.
Following pages: Wehrmacht cavalrymen passing through a
village burnt by the SS during the German advance into Russia.

TO THE FOUR
CORNERS
OF THE WORLD

Anti-Semitic Germany denouncing
the invasion of Jews fleeing the Tsar.

498

Lottery ticket of the O.Z.E.T. (a society to aid Jewish workers in the USSR to become farmers)
dated May 1st, 1928, a few days before the arrival of the first group of colonists in Tikonkaya, later
the town of Birobidzan. This attempt to establish an autonomous Jewish republic had several aims:
to serve as buffer territory between the Soviet Union and the Far Eastern powers; to regenerate, through
work on the land, Jews whose "bourgeois mentality and unproductive role" was deplored by the Soviet
government; to fortify their nationality by uniting them around a common denominator, Yiddish,
which had become a propaganda instrument for the regime. This ersatz Zionism was a resounding failure.

Soviet propaganda for Birobidzan.
"The departure of Jewish labor to work in Kuznekstroj."

The Jewish region of Stalindorf.
"**A** meeting of workers of the brigades of the Kolkhoz to increase efficiency."
Opposite: "Children of repatriated Jewish immigrants."
"**A**n international delegation of Birobidzan pioneers from the Belorussian Republic."

502

BIRO BIDJAN — RUSSIAN JEWISH COLONY — ASIA

Birobidzan, Valdgeim kolkhoz. "One of the best teams." "Working in a field of vegetables."

Crimean Republic. "A Jewish worker during a rest period." The "Without God" agricultural kolkhoz.

"**A** Birobidzan airplane flying over the national regions of Russia, Ukraine and Crimea."
Opposite: the Bezboznick kolkhoz in the Stalindorf region. "In the background, the repair area."

"**A** group of pioneers from Korea and China."
Opposite: the spa town of Kuldur. "The pavilion over a spring."

Jediný polský
export.

"The only Polish export": emigrants, attracted particularly by work in the mines of northern France. This hemorrhage of manpower was generally attributed to bad government. The anti-Semitic movements had naturally blamed it on the Jews. **O**pposite: Russian and Romanian Jews "invading" the Vienna of anti-Semitic mayor Karl Lueger.

Die Juden geh'n im Gänsemarsch
Was haben sie im Sinn?
So zog'n sie übers rothe Meer
Der Wolf, der Fuchs, der Löw, der Beer
Die Juden geh'n im Gänsemarsch
Zum Lueger nach Wien.

509

2/2/1906.

Gruss aus Prag!

Das jüdische Rathaus. — 62.

J'envoie a chacun de vous une carte
d'un appartement a m' Florentin les jours
passé où je vous embrasse tous les trois
en attendant...

The old cemetery in Prague, a necropolis of twelve thousand souls.
Opposite: in the foreground, Europe's oldest synagogue, the Altneuschul in Prague,
built in 1270. In the background, the Jewish Town Hall, whose clock face has Hebraic
numerals and whose hands turn in the opposite direction to those of traditional clocks.

512

Anti-Semitic depictions of Viennese Jews at the turn of the century.
Opposite: Jews from the countryside flocking to the city of hope.

Galizische Bevölkerung.
Juden aus der Provinz.

514

Vienna. Galicians talking on a street corner.

A kosher restaurant in the center of Berlin, frequented by the traditionalist elite of German Judaism.

Herr Kommerzienrat!

Berlin im Zeichen
des Fortschritts!

Freie Bahn dem Tüchtigen!

Photographs taken in the Jewish quarter in Berlin. Their ironic captions attempt to underline the long road remaining for these orthodox Jews before they become integrated into the German people.

518

Yiddishland in the heart of Berlin.

520

Here, Yiddish is spoken, not German.

Rembrandt's house in the Jewish quarter of Amsterdam.

I. J. ASSCHER – AMSTERDAM, TOLSTRAAT 127–129

The imposing diamond cutting factory belonging to the Asher family, renowned for its fight for social justice and militancy in favor of the underprivileged in the Amsterdam community.

Momentopname uit het Amsterdamsche Straatleven

WE USE
THE MASTER
WATERPROOF
BOOT POLISH

Amsterdam

„Izak" de schoenpoet
van den Dam

Izak, the famous Amsterdam shoe shiner.
Following pages: Amsterdam's Jewish quarter.

Amsterdam

In den Jodenhoek. "Levendige Ling"

וְכָל בָּנַיִךְ לִמּוּדֵי ה

Children in the *heder* in Amsterdam, "Jerusalem of the north".
Opposite: Jozef Israels, Dutch painter influenced both by Rembrandt and by the Barbizon School. He was particularly interested in the common people, fishermen and peasants, portrayed in the romantic mists of his country.

No. 5. Jan Veth

Jozef Israels

יוסף ישראלים

THE JEWISH JOURNAL

The OSBORN PUBLISHING Co.,
LESSEES OF THE JEWISH PRESS LT
40, OSBORN STREET,

CLOSED
ON SATURDAYS. London....21 - 6....191 2

The Yiddish press in London.
Opposite: Yiddish theater in the land of Shakespeare.

THE GHETTO. LONDON,

Sunday morning in the Jewish quarter of London.
Following pages: Jewish life in all its intensity in Petticoat Lane, London.

GLOVES
AND
HOSIERY
Every Pair Guaranteed

PETTICOAT LANE   WENTWORTH STREET

536

Sunday morning in Middlesex Street, Petticoat Lane.

Editions de la Société Cinématographique
RENE FERNAND
61, rue de Chabrol, Paris-X

538

Une scène du film « METAMORPHOSES »
qui sera joué au Palais de la Mutualité - Cinéma -
325, rue St-Martin, du 15 au 21 février.

Une scène du film « MÉTAMORPHOSES » qui sera joué au Palais de la Mutualité - Cinéma - 325, rue St-Martin, du 8 au 14 février.

539

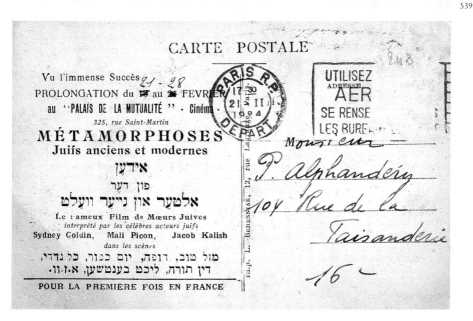

The Yiddish Cinema in Paris (1934).

Kosher butchers proud of their difference and their role in enabling
practicing Jews to respect the culinary prescriptions of the Law.

542

325. - PARIS
Le Marché du Temple. - G I.

From the 19th century onwards, refugees from numerous countries thronged to the Carreau du Temple, a giant covered market built in the style of Baltard, where the majority of traders were Jewish.

829   Marchés de Paris (Marché du Temple). — Marchands Fripiers

ND Phot

544

Ritual slaughter of a bull by a *shohet* (sacrificer) in the old abattoir at La Villette, Paris.

Paris artistique et pittoresque

Paris IVme - Rue des Hospitalières St-Gervais - Ecoles communales et Laboratoire municipal de micrographie
Doit son nom à un ancien Couvent de Religieuses

Rue des Hospitalières Saint-Gervais in the Pletzl, the Jewish quarter in Paris's 4th arrondissement.

1123   PARIS. — Rue Eugène-Sue. — ND Phot.

Only by chance did this kosher restaurant open in rue Eugène Sue in Montmartre, Paris. Sue was the author of *The Wandering Jew*, a famous novel published fifty years earlier; it is as if, by abandoning the traditional Jewish quarter, the restaurant's owners had been branded by the curse of the eternal wanderer.

2407. PARIS - Rue des Rosiers

Gondry, édit Paris

Rue des Rosiers, the heart of Paris's Pletzl.

550

Rue des Hospitalières Saint-Gervais in Paris's Pletzl quarter.

2401. PARIS - Rue des Rosiers   Gondry, édit. Paris

The Pletzl at the beginning of the 20th century: rue des Rosiers, Paris.

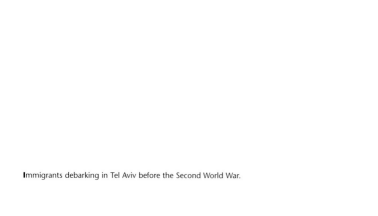

Immigrants debarking in Tel Aviv before the Second World War.

On deck on the *Palestine*, sailing towards the Promised Land in the 1930s.

The *SS Polonia* sailed continuously back and forth between Poland and Israel.

JERUSALEM, Mea Saharim.　　　　　　　　　　　　　　　ירושלים, מאה שערים

In Mea Shearim, the quarter of the orthodox Jews in Jerusalem, most of the inhabitants spoke Yiddish rather than Hebrew.
Opposite: daily life in Jerusalem.

Bei den Auswandererhallen Hamburg.

559

German Jews gathered at the emigration center in Hamburg in the 1930s.

560

Russian Jews waiting for the official stamp of the American administration allowing them entry into Paradise.
Opposite: the sorting center on Ellis Island, in Upper New York Bay, the entry point of millions of immigrants into America.

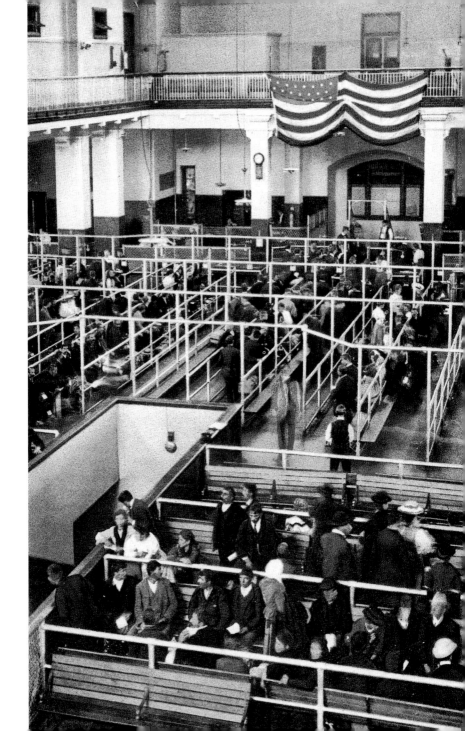

The Yiddish press in the United States, representative of all movements.

אויסגאבען פֿון די סאצ.-טעריט. 1902-1907.

YIDDISH
ART
THEATRE
MAURICE SCHWARTZ
Director

7th AVENUE
at 59th STREET

Tel. CIrcle
6-1730

NOW PLAYING
EVENINGS 8:30
Incl. SUNDAYS
MATINEES
SAT. & SUN. 2:30

 266

MAURICE SCHWARTZ and SAMUEL GOLDENBERG
as the **BROTHERS ASHKENAZI**

564

JORDAN & HARVEY
America's Greatest Hebrew Dialect Comedians

Maurice Schwartz and Samuel Goldenberg as the Brothers Ashkenazi, adapted from the famous work by Israel Joshua Singer.
The duetists Jordan and Harvey, proud to continue the tradition of the Yiddish *shtetl*.
Opposite: the Yiddish actor Menasha Skulnik (born in Warsaw in 1892), during a performance of *Flowering Sin*.

568

A Pickle Vender in the Ghetto
New York City

Traders in the New York "ghetto".
Preceding pages: second-hand clothes market, Baxter Street, New York.

*Ghetto
New York*

In the Jewish quarter in New York, one is American but one thinks, speaks and sells in Yiddish.
Following pages: the Lower East Side, New York's "ghetto".

574

Little Jerusalem.

Daily life in the Jewish quarter of New York.

Essex & Hester St.
New York

The corner of Essex and Hester Streets.

Buenos Aires. The reception center for European immigrants. In 1899, as soon as he came ashore, Enrique Dickmann, a militant socialist, wrote: "Nobody asked me who I was or where I came from."

Recuerdo de Buenos Aires

CASA DE INMIGRANTES

27 — J. PEUSER, BS. AS.

ASILO INFANTIL ISRAELITA PARA NIÑAS (Propiedad de la Sociedad de Socorros de Damas Israelitas)

בית יתומות פון דעם אידישען דאמען הילפס-פאראיין

581

HOSPITAL ISRAELITA "EZRAH"
FRENTE PRINCIPAL

Gaona 2801
Buenos Aires

A refuge for children run by the Aid Society of Israelite Women, created in 1904 in Rosario.
A hospital in Buenos Aires run by the Ezrah Israelite Charitable and Mutual Help Society, inaugurated in 1920.
Opposite: the first congress of Argentinian Jews, presided over by Natan Gesang.

582

The synagogue in Harbin in Chinese Manchuria, built by Russian Jews.

(ハルビン)　鋪道に映くロシヤ美人（B）
Russian girls (Harbin)

Russian Jews promenading in the streets of Harbin.

The Jewish School in Pretoria.
One of the three synagogues in Durban.
Opposite: 'Doctor' Cohen, one of the pioneer emigrants to South Africa.

Mr. G. COHN, one of the Pioneers of the Rand.
To his Patrons he is known as "Jacob". Mr. Cohn is nearly 80 years of age,
is a bird-fancier, doctor, linguist, photographer, produce and curio-dealer,
market agent &c.

SELECT BIBLIOGRAPHY

ALGEMAYNE ENTSYKLOPEDIE,
11 volumes, Cyko, New York, 1935-1948.

BAUMGARTEN Jean, *Introduction à la littérature yiddish ancienne*, Le Cerf, 1993.

BAUMGARTEN Jean, *Le Yiddish*, Presses universitaires de France, 1990.

CZERNIAKOW Adam, *Carnets du ghetto de Varsovie*, La Découverte, 1996.

DAWIDOWICZ Lucy, *La Guerre contre les Juifs*, Hachette, 1997.

DICTIONNAIRE ENCYCLOPÉDIQUE DU JUDAÏSME (collectif), Le Cerf, 1993.

DOBZYNSKI Charles, *Le Miroir d'un peuple*, Gallimard, 1971.

DOBZYNSKI Charles, *Le Monde du yiddish*, L'Harmattan, 1998.

DOUBNOV Simon, *Histoire moderne du peuple juif, 1789-1938*, Le Cerf, 1994.

ERTEL Rachel, *Dans la langue de personne, poésie yiddish de l'anéantissement*, Éditions du Seuil, 1993.

ERTEL Rachel, *Le Shtetl. La bourgade juive de Pologne*, Payot, 1982.

GUGENHEIM Ernest, *Le Judaïsme dans la vie quotidienne*, Albin Michel, 1978.

HILBERG Raul, *La Destruction des Juifs d'Europe*, Fayard, 1988.

HOWE Irving, *Le Monde de nos pères*, Michalon, 1997.

KLATZMANN Joseph, *L'humour juif*, Presses universitaires de France, 1998.

KOCHAN Lionel (sous la direction de), *Les Juifs en Union soviétique depuis 1918*, Calmann-Lévy, 1971.

KORZEC Pawel, *Juifs en Pologne*, Fondation nationale ès sciences politiques, 1980.

LAQUEUR Walter, *Histoire du sionisme*, Calmann-Lévy, 1973.

LITUANIE JUIVE. MESSAGE D'UN MONDE ENGLOUTI, 1918-1940 (collectif), Autrement, 1996.

MILLE ANS DE CULTURES ASHKÉNAZES (collectif), Liana Levi, 1994.

MILOSZ Czeslaw, *Une Autre Europe*, Gallimard, 1964.

MINCZELES Henri, *Histoire générale du Bund, un mouvement révolutionnaire juif*, Austral, 1995.

MINCZELES Henri, *Vilna, Wilno, Vilnius. La Jérusalem de Lituanie*, La Découverte, 1993.

NIBORSKI Itzhok, WIEVIORKA Annette, *Les Livres du souvenir, mémoriaux juifs de Pologne*, Gallimard, 1983.

RAN Leizer, *Yerushalayim de Lita*, 3 volumes, Laureate Press, 1982.

ROBIN Régine, *L'Amour du yiddish, écriture juive et sentiment de la langue, 1830-1930*, Sorbier, 1984.

SILVAIN Gérard, *Images et Traditions juives*, Astrid, 1980.

SILVAIN Gérard, *Deux Destins en Diaspora*, Albin Michel, 1984.

TOLLET Daniel, *Les Juifs en Pologne du xvie siècle à nos jours*, Presses universitaires de France, 1992.

TRAVERSO Enzo, *Les Marxistes et la Question juive*, Éditions de La Brèche, 1990.

WEINSTOCK Nathan, *Le Pain de misère*, 3 tomes, La Découverte, 1984-1986.

ZBOROWSKI Mark, HERZOG Élisabeth, *Olam*, Plon, 1992.

587